PUBLIC SPEAKING
IS A SPORT

PUBLIC SPEAKING IS A SPORT

A motivational perspective of a sportsman

IQBAL RANA, DTM

Library of Congress Control Number: 2019900015
Paperback ISBN: 9781793030269
Public Speaking is a Sport - First Edition

ACKNOWLEDGEMENTS

I would like to acknowledge my lovely wife, Ghazala, who is the best thing that happened to me in this life. She provides me guidance and support in everything I do. I cannot practically spend hours playing sports during weekdays and weekends without her support and understanding. She is always the first person to listen to my speeches and provides most constructive feedback. She suggested several critical ideas during the writing of this book and helped me in putting both of my passions together.

My beautiful daughter Mutahira, who reviewed and provided several suggestions for improvement in grammar and layout of the book.

My dear sons Bilal and Hamood, who took major task of editing this book. Editing a book of an immigrant from a non-English speaking country, cannot be easy so I applaud their effort and patience.

Lastly, my parents who passed away in 1991, but they asked us to stay connected, stay grounded and keep dreaming big.

TABLE OF CONTENTS

A FOREWORD

There are hundreds of books written on the topic of public speaking, why another book? Some of you must be thinking that public speaking most definitely is not a sport and there must be something else in this book, maybe it is merely an analogy?

The author of this book was looking for something that he could personally relate to. Born with a talent of table tennis, a competitive spirit and a strong desire to be an articulate and confident one, he was searching for books that could motivate him. During his search, he found public speaking books that were wonderfully written, but they said the same things in different writing styles. At the same time, he was running into many arguments about what a sport really was? Is beer pong a sport, is golf a sport and is poker a sport since it involves one's face from giving away their hand? Are race car drivers athletes? Are mountain climbers sportsmen? Reading all these suggestions about how to become a good speaker and what really is a sport, the author decided to tackle both issues with this book and hopes you will enjoy and learn.

Public speaking remains to be a challenge that we all must overcome to express ourselves the best we can. Our ability to speak can help us win hearts at work, in our community, among our friends and family and not to mention it may help us win the heart to spend rest of our lives with. We all get nervous especially when it is a moment that matters to us the most, an interview, an introduction to an audience or a presentation to executives. Mark Twain said, "There are two types of speakers: Those who get nervous and those who are liars". In simple translation, it means we all get nervous. Even the most popular speakers worry about subpar performance despite of their experience.

This book intends to provide tools and techniques to overcome the nervousness that any speaker may feel. It offers beginner and intermediate level speakers to find their own analogies and passions to compare with public speaking, even if they don't play or watch sports

ABOUT THE AUTHOR

Iqbal Rana is a Distinguished Toastmaster (DTM) who has been an area director, president, vice president of education and member of Toastmasters International for over 7 years in Orange County and San Diego County, California. Iqbal has won several speaking contests and has spoken to large audiences at national and state levels. When Iqbal joined toastmasters club, he was at a level of speaking where he would start shaking if his name was called from the podium with a fear that he may have to say something in front of many in attendance. It is safe to say that Iqbal was NOT born with a natural talent of public speaking.

While Iqbal was not born with speaking talent, he was born with a natural talent in table tennis and a competitive nature for any sport he played including volleyball, tennis, badminton, cricket, taekwondo and even tug of war. As a table tennis player Iqbal won many tournaments and championships in front of large crowds and sometimes in situations where almost whole crowd was rooting for his opponent. Additionally, as a martial arts enthusiast, Iqbal holds black belt in Kukkiwon discipline of taekwondo.

Iqbal was born in Pakistan, an Asian country where it is responsibility of the listener to understand and not the speaker to make sure the message is properly delivered. Having lived in Canada and USA for most of his life, he learnt that, in this culture, the onus is on the speaker to deliver the message, so it could be understood. This major cultural shift encouraged Iqbal to change his mindset and improve his public speaking skills to stay competitive.

In this book, Iqbal will share a perspective of a natural sportsman who became a public speaker by simply working hard like a sportsman, routinely practicing and constantly working to improve himself.

This book addresses anyone who has a competitive drive and passion to tackle his/her fear of public speaking.

PART ONE

We all have dreams, but what separates the achievers from the losers is conviction and a roadmap. If you want to become a public speaker, then name your goal and write down a plan of how you will get there. Top athletes and public speakers don't simply walk into a competition without practice and prior planning.

This part covers everything you do **before** a sports match and what you should do before you find yourself behind the podium and facing the audience. More than half of the battle is decided before it even begins. This will show that you control your own destiny because of the work that goes in preparing for the moment.

Chapter 1

SPORTS vs. PUBLIC SPEAKING

Human beings have been playing sports for as long as they have existed. Not only do we play sports to remain healthy, but also for our personal entertainment.

According to Britannica,

"No one can say when sports began. Since it is impossible to imagine a time when children did not spontaneously run races or wrestle, children have always included sports in their play."

This tells us that we invented sports as our human society progressed in time. This was done for entertainment, social bonding and health.

Let's look at how sports can have a relationship with public speaking.

"Play- wrote the German theorist Carl Diem, "is purpose-less activity, for its own sake, the opposite of work." Humans work because they have to; they play because they want to. There are at least two types of play. Spontaneous, where a child sees a flat stone, picks it up, and sends it skipping across the waters of a pond. Second type of play is an organized play, where rules are defined to determine which actions are legitimate and which are not. Organized games can further be refined into non-competitive games like leap frog and playing house where no one wins versus competitive games like Chess and Basketball." Britannica

Now that we are at the point of separating competitive sports vs competitive games, we could safely say that any play requiring physical effort would be considered a sport while an intellectual contest would not. However, we can see how close public speaking is to a sport. Well, we may not call public speaking a sport, but let's play along to see how, being familiar with sports can help us become a good public speaker.

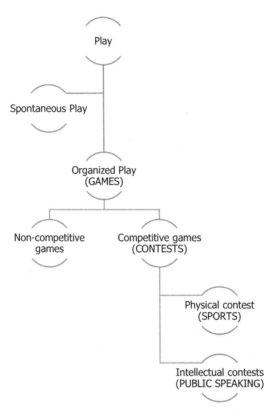

The inverted tree shows a relation of public speaking with sports which begins with a very innate nature of humans to play. We play for our enjoyment, we play to socialize, and we play to find our place in the society. Politics is one big example of a game. We play politics with other human beings and other societies to build partnerships and sometimes alliances to fight our opponents. Many wars in human history have been fought because of miscommunications and many alliances were built to meet political objectives. As humans we are always involved in physical and intellectual contests. Looking at the inverted tree above, we start to see how both types of contests come together and how they are important for our survival.

PHYSICAL AND INTELLECTUAL CONTESTS

Here is side by side comparison of sports (physical play) with public speaking (intellectual play) to show how closely they are related.

Sports	Public Speaking
Physical and mental health	Mental health
Team work and social connections	Social connections
Improved self esteem	Improved self esteem
Chances of career and academic growth	Higher chances of career and academic growth
Enhanced energy	Enhanced communication skills
Competitive nature and strong desire to win	Competitive nature and strong desire to inspire
Enjoyment	Possible enjoyment*

* Public speaking may itself be very rewarding and enjoyable if the speaker feels that he/she can make a difference or change the direction of a thought.

Unfortunately, ability to articulate and present your thoughts better can also be used against vulnerable humans. For example, some managers and their subordinates in the corporate world, may build their careers by simply being articulate and they may not feel the need to work hard. They may even take credit for work that someone else did and enjoy their career success that way. Such colleagues may enjoy their careers, but they are clearly neither leaders nor team players.

Looking at side by side comparison in the table above, we see how close sports are to public speaking. My own journey from sports to public speaking was driven by how easy it was as a sportsman to stay healthy, enjoy the time and still reap many other benefits. My competitive nature as a sportsman told me that I must carve out my own destiny and that is exactly what I wanted to do with public speaking.

Let's review in greater detail how sports can guide us to becoming better public speakers.

*LIFE IS A GAME AND
WE MUST BE SOCIALLY
COMPETITIVE
TO SURVIVE*

Chapter 2

HIT THE GYM

When we want to stay active or we want to live a healthier lifestyle, the very first thought we have is to, start doing exercise. We could very well decide to do a daily short walk, jog a mile or join a gym to build our muscles and stay fit.

For sportspersons, the gym offers them a place to get in shape and prepare their bodies for sport they choose to play. If they are marathon runners, they may choose to use the treadmill to practice running, stationary bikes if they are bikers, free weights if they are boxers or wrestlers and they may very well use all these tools in moderation to build body strength in order to play their sport the best they can.

Sportspersons and non-sportspersons alike, go to the gym and do regular exercise for following reasons.

* Exercise increases their energy level
  * They can perform at a higher level and make their team and boss happy
  * They can do more home chores and make their mom or their "real boss" happy
  * Gives them energy to play more with their children, nephews and nieces
  * Helps them stay active during a monotonous speech or college lecture they don't like
* Allows them to build the right muscles
  * Increases physical strength in the areas being focused. Most gym members exercise for every muscle in their body however men may focus more on biceps and ladies may focus on toning of their legs
  * Helps heart muscle to become more efficient and better able to pump blood throughout the body
* Helps avoid medication and frequent visits to the doctor
  * Exercise helps keep their arteries and veins clear from blockage
  * Reduces chances of diabetes, heart problems and many other diseases
  * Allows them to enjoy healthier life until the last minute and not drag themselves to a bigger age number.
* They may want to lose weight
  * Controlled weight allows them to feel more agile and nimble

* They feel better for
  • Themselves, their teams, friends, family and community

Before we discuss how these reasons relate to public speaking, let's review few more points of how going to the gym is a critical contributing factor for a sportsperson's success.

Almost every sportsperson who plays at world class, national, state or college level sports goes to a gym, even if he/she has tools in his/her garage. They all go to the gym to build muscles required to play the sport they are already good at. They do cardio, strength, flexibility, balance exercises and much more, to prepare themselves for their respective sport. Many of them join sporting gyms because it offers them a safe place to do exercise and an atmosphere that motivates them to do more. Additionally, some gym members and especially competitive athletes hire fitness coaches to help them work on right muscles, so they can work towards a given goal without hurting or overexerting themselves.

Now let me ask you, do you remember the first time when you walked into a gym? Walking into a gym for the first time may have been a very intimidating experience. You can be intimidated by the number of people, tools available and maybe the whole atmosphere. You may see some guys with biceps that are bigger than your thighs and perfectly figured gals who seem to have it all. This atmosphere may send some newcomers back home. However, as an athlete you know that it is very possible that those perfectly made men and women may have been members of the gym for a long period of time or maybe they were born with toned bodies and they are there to perfect what they already have. As an athlete you feel a sense of competition in this atmosphere and a need to work hard. Your hard work depends on your natural talent, current level and your ambitions. For example, Tom Brady, who is the most decorated quarterback in the history of American football, can pass the ball to his team members with pin point accuracy. But, if he is asked to play soccer and pass a soccer ball with such accuracy, it will be much more difficult. He may work very hard but his accuracy may still not match Lionel Messi or any other top soccer player. This example shows that your level of effort and how far you will be successful, depends on your natural talent and the hard work you put in.

These arguments show that competitive sportspersons go to a gym to prepare their bodies for the sport of their choice. They are not intimidated by the atmosphere, instead they work harder to get better than their competition Now let's see if same concept applies to public speaking and if there is a gym for public speaking.

PUBLIC SPEAKING GYM

While sports are critical for our physical fitness, being able to speak and present ourselves better is also as critical for our survival in this jungle of social animals. Humans are social animals and we want to communicate more expressively as opposed to other animals. For example: A dog will only bark a couple of different ways but will mostly use its body language to show how much he loves you. Humans on the other hand, use not only body language but cry, laugh, smile, scream and use millions of words to express themselves. And yes, some may even have choice words to express themselves, but I guess you get the point.

If you want to be able to communicate better and you were not born with a public speaking talent, then it will take you more work to get better. Most of us are not born with all talents at once, so we must work harder in areas where we want to excel.

Public speaking like staying healthy cannot be done by sitting at home or by simply walking to the stage and hoping that you will knock it out of the park. You will need to get out of your comfort zone. You will need to do some exercise to be able to communicate better.

Let's look at the benefits of exercising for public speaking and note similarities with physical exercise mentioned above.

* Increases your energy level
    • You feel more confident in any social setting
    • You may become the life of a party
* You feel better
    • By expressing feelings more appropriately
    • You may get more chances of being successful in your career if you can present better, speak better and motivate your audiences to action
* Allows you to build the right muscles
    • You build your speaking muscles and find easier to communicate
    • Stimulates your brain muscles that help you speak

* Lose "weight"

- Well, you may not lose your physical weight, you can lift a major weight off your shoulders if you said what you wanted to say for a long time. I suggest using caution in taking the weight off too quickly.

* Avoid medication

- Humans feel stress when they are not able to express themselves during changing life events like challenges of a new job, loss of a long-held job, passing of a family member or an illness or injury. Major life changes may bring you significant stress, however being able to express yourselves may alleviate this stress.

Now that we know benefits of public speaking exercise, where are the gyms for such exercise? There are many types of public speaking "gyms" available around us. High schoolers, as an example, can start at clubs with assigned teachers where coaches can provide guidance. For example, the Junior State of America (JSA) club. JSA is a non-partisan youth organization. The purpose of JSA is to help high school students acquire leadership skills and the knowledge necessary to be effective debaters and civic participants. Other organizations such as Toastmasters International and Pure Potentials provide opportunities to learn and improve your public speaking skills.

Toastmasters International is a US headquartered non-profit educational organization that operates clubs worldwide for promoting communication and public speaking skills. It has over 90 years of history. You can join a Toastmasters club by looking at your closest Toastmasters club in the area at www.toastmasters.org.

Pure Potentials Speakers Clubs create communities where you can sharpen your speaking skills. You can visit https://pure-potentials.com/ for more information about this organization.

Just like sports gyms, there could potentially be many speaking clubs near you. While sports gyms allow opportunities and atmosphere for fitness of body and mind, public speaking clubs offer the same for fitness of speech. For examples, Toastmasters clubs offer a safe place to practice public speaking skills and build speaking muscles. You may fail many times before you succeed however you will consistently find an atmosphere of encouragement no matter where in the world you join this club. There will always be outstanding speakers, but you will not be able to tell whether they practiced this skill through speaking organizations for many years or if they are simply there to perfect their innate talents. These clubs provide all the tools necessary to become a successful speaker, such as coaches, mentors, and several other resources to ensure you are on the right track

Sports gyms and public speaking clubs offer opportunities for you to work hard to meet your long-term goals and offer a safe place to sharpen your muscles and skills and get motivated at the same time. Miquel Cotto said, "The harder I train every day on the track and in the gym, the more trust I gain in myself." You will most definitely gain more trust in yourself the more you practice.

There is a saying for physical fitness that you do not have an hour for exercise today, but when you get sick you will have many hours every day to take care of your illness. The same applies to public speaking. For example, you do not want to start practicing your ability to interview after you have lost your job. Likewise, you do not want to start learning how to speak in front of management after you have already started a job. As you can see, both problems are risky, however they can be solved with just a few hours of public speaking practice every week. Therefore, you must keep your physical and mental muscles engaged, so you can be ready in any situation.

No matter how strong or weak you feel in your public speaking skills, just know that all high school to world class athletes are working out at the gym to prepare their bodies for the game they choose to play. Public speakers should also find opportunities to work out their body muscles, so their mind, tongue, and body can work in unison. Unlike gyms, where you must go three to five times a week to meet your goals, an hour to two hours a week in public speaking clubs will be more than enough to get you going. With all that said, I highly recommend joining a public speaking club and if you are serious then please do not wait for a New Year resolution.

EXERCISE:
Choose best answer to face your fear of public speaking. Hint: Option 3 and 4 maybe quite similar

1. Walk to a stage and wing it
2. Join a public speaking club

3. Make a resolution for the next year
4. Do nothing

LEARNING:
You never achieve anything in life by dreaming or simply having a hope. You will need to follow a routine to become a public speaker

PUBLIC SPEAKING CLUBS
PROVIDE YOU A PLACE
FOR FITNESS OF SPEECH

Chapter 3

HAVE A GAME PLAN

In our normal lives, we plan for every important activity, so we can successfully meet our defined objectives. Competitive sportspersons make detailed plan when they are preparing to play competitive game against another team. Going to a gym allowed them to prep their bodies however their preparation goes beyond the gym where they were focused only on toning of their bodies. Now, they need to go beyond the gym and must plan for the successful execution of their end goal.

Planning of a sportsperson includes:

* Reviewing of opposing players and their coach
  • Watching videos of their competitor
  • Discussing their prior matches with opponents
  • Discussing strengths and weaknesses of their opponent as well as their own

* Plan for weather and field conditions
  * Wear appropriate gear
  * Plan to pace their game based on conditions
* Discussing the type of audience
* Discussing motivational factors of why this match is important
* Planning for what to eat or drink before and during the game
* Planning for time
  * Ensure timely arrival through guaranteed/safe means
  * Align your pace of game for time allotted to the game
* Review last-minute practice and relaxation plans
* Review backup plan during execution
  * Pack extra gear that may be needed
  * Include extra players that maybe needed
  * Prepare responses to different play patterns

If I intend to play volleyball with co-workers on a given Wednesday, I cannot afford to forget putting my sporting gear in my car. Not only do I have to bring all necessary items, I must also make sure that the rest of my team does the same. California may always have nice weather, but I must keep an extra jacket to be safe. Lastly, I should eat something before 5 PM so I can perform during the game. All of us must do this very simple level of planning, even for the simplest of the games we choose to play on regular basis

This is a discipline that applies to every match played by every sports enthusiast. The more challenging their game level, the more they must prepare. I may forget a bottle of water for my volleyball game but if I make the slightest mistake in my preparation for my competitive match, it may affect my whole team. If it is an individual sport, then I may put myself at non-competitive situation. In other words, if I do not prepare for my match in advance, I may set myself or my team for failure before the game even begins. Planning and preparation are essential part of any sport.

HOW DOES A GAME PLAN APPLY TO PUBLIC SPEAKING?

Public speaking is just like any sports game in our life, it cannot be executed without a game plan. You should plan for every speaking engagement just as you do for sports because you cannot afford to show yourselves ill prepared and show an unsportsmanlike like conduct.

Stephen Covey's 7 habits of highly effective people provide an excellent guideline for preparing yourselves for success.

1. Be proactive
    *   You must have an inner desire that is supported by effort. For example, you want to win hearts and minds of people through your speaking skills, so you join a club to perfect your art of public speaking.

2. Begin with an end in mind
   - When you join a club, make sure you have a specific high goal in mind and have a plan to reach the goal. For example, you want to speak at a major technical conference or a community meeting or maybe speak at a TED hosted event.
3. Put first things first
   - Prioritize your desire of public speaking along with all other needs and desires in life. For example, you have professional and family life, hobbies you partake in, sports you play, gym you go to and you wish to be an eloquent speaker. Therefore, you must add speech practice to your list of commitments
4. Think win/win
   - You do not have to lose one hobby to achieve another. Manage your time well and its possible you could contribute in all hobbies and needs of life to a reasonable degree. For example, ask yourself if it is important to sit a bit longer in a coffee shop with a friend or use that time for a hobby that adds more value to your life? Is it important to have lunch with same colleagues every day or can you sometimes use that hour to go to a gym or a public speaking club? Is it possible to have working lunch and use the saved time to leave early from work and fulfill a more important need after work? Answers to these questions may help you plan for a win/win situation.

5. Seek first to understand, then be understood
   - In my view, this is the most critical point for speaking to an audience. You are there to serve the needs of the audience, so it is very important that you understand their needs first before you suggest any solution or advice. A good speaker's job is not to lecture but provide information and/or call for action.
6. Synergize
   - It is important for a good speaker to put himself/herself at the level of the audience and align with their needs and understand their differences. Once this is done, you have built their trust thus creating synergy resulting in a whole that is greater than some of its parts.
7. Sharpen the saw
   - This is when practice becomes a critical component of your plan and your focus shifts only to perfecting what you desired. The more you practice the more you sound confident and authentic.

When we speak in front of others, we are clearly exposed, and all our imperfections seem to amplify. Suppose you simply forget to comb your hair one day and you realize just before the presentation to executives and at this point you do not even have access to a brush? In this state, you have not even stepped into the meeting room. You are already scrambling, and you might even have to go in with your "scrambled" hair. You would already be feeling low in confidence to present while you have not even started talking yet.

Proper planning before any speech and presentation will give you a nice head start to your presentation. Dressing up nicely and appropriate to audience needs, will boost your confidence while it is not even part of the talk you prepared.

WHAT SHOULD YOU PLAN ABOUT?

Planning for speech depends on the type of speech or presentation and it also depends on the type of audience you are presenting to. Speaker speaking at a public community meeting may be very animated in their speech, but they may have a completely different tone of speech when speaking to a conservative audience. If you are presenting to executive leadership, you may have to calibrate your speech according to every individual member. Sometimes, you will direct your speech to one of the members, who possibly asks most of the tough questions to satisfy needs of that executive. In short, you must plan your presentation based on what you are presenting and who you are presenting to.

For a successful presentation or speech, you should do following:

* Review and understand expectations from those who asked us to speak.
  • Review other speech competitors or speakers on the same forum

- Watch videos of prior events and speakers who might be speaking at the event
- See how you will be different and more meaningful

* Review the audience and type of gathering
  - Executives, sports teams, conservatives, liberals, teenagers, baby boomers, students and teachers to name a few.
  - Trainees and students are example of friendly audience. However, a political audience and prospect customer presentations may be examples of hostile audiences.

* Be an early bird
  - Arriving early will allow you to build rapport with audience members who are already there
  - Allows you to review the environment before the speech
  - Avoids stress that can be caused by being late

* Review the stage positioning, lighting and audio arrangements in the room
  - An auditorium will require a different mindset versus a raised stage versus a meeting room
  - Lights and sound systems can change everything about how a speech may have been prepared

* Clear your throat and avoid dryness
  - Avoid dry or cold food
  - Sips of a hot drink may help

* Plan to relax, smile and stretch before the speech
  - Smiling will release mental stress

- Stretching will relax tense muscles
* Execute a backup plan if the original plan does not work out
  - Bring a printed copy of your speech for yourself
  - Bring printed copies for attendees if it's a small group
  - Prepare plan if microphone fails or lights go out
  - How will you handle distracted audience member or members?
  - Plan to avoid panic situations that might arise
  - Know that you can never win by blaming audience
* Write with a goal in mind
  - Start by engaging your audience, deliver your message and leave them with something they will remember

No speech should be conducted without going through all the details required to execute a speech. You can try doing the same speech with two different audience types and you will realize that one audience maybe more receptive to your message versus other audience. Always remember philosophy of different strokes for different folks. One group may have tolerance for your humor while the other may not. One group may understand your underlying message, but the other group may not. You can also try delivering the same speech with and without microphone and you will see how significantly it changes your plan for vocal variety. It may also limit body gestures if it is attached to the podium. or it may limit your hand gestures if you are holding the microphone. Bottomline, you must plan every speech for each setting in mind.

One of my speech contests, had audience seated at the same level as the speakers so I was able to walk closer to the audience and have conversation of sorts. The next round contest had an elevated stage where I had to look down at my audience with spotlights hitting directly on my eyes and yet another speech was in auditorium setting where I had to look up at my audience which tired out my neck muscles forcing me to look down to rest during my pauses. Every stage type presented me with its own challenges and opportunities though I was delivering the same speech that I practiced so many times. The audience does not care whether you are being blinded by spot lights, having challenges with microphone or your neck is getting tired. You will need to find ways to counter all those environmental challenges before you execute your speech. As you can see, this emphasizes the importance of planning ahead.

WRITE WITH PURPOSE

Writing a speech, unsurprisingly, is the most critical part of your planning process. Interestingly, some of world's most famous speeches were simply read from a paper, but they had the biggest impact. These are exceptions not the rule. I can at least tell you, many formal US presidential speeches are practiced many times before they are delivered by reading from the teleprompter. One of my favorite speeches was Steve Jobs' (CEO of Apple) 2005 Stanford commencement address where

Steve Jobs read a speech that was written with most powerful and most meaningful stories from his own life. While I don't know how much he practiced reading the speech, but he did spend time to write a very impactful speech.

When writing speeches, know that one speech style does not fit all. Preparation is everything and it starts with understanding expectations. You can deliver best speech of your life and you finished it on time, but if it did not meet expectations of the audience, then it failed. In project management world, many project managers will take pride in completing projects on time and on budget, but was this the only criteria asked for? A contractor may build your house within your budget and schedule but if you do not like the shades of color they painted, then will you be happy? Probably not, because they should have consulted you before completing the paint job. The same applies to delivering a speech at any forum where you have been hired to deliver a message. You must deliver what you are expected to by your host, and your audience.

Write your speech after understanding the requirements of the host and expectations of the audience. Type of the audience should always be kept in mind because though most of the time your audience will be a mixture of male and female however it could very well be just one gender type, it may have certain political or religious affiliation depending on city/state or county you are speaking in, or it may be all young or all old.

A good written speech will always:

* Be relevant, organized and written for the audience
* Use simple sentences, even if it is a technical presentation

* Have a story constantly moving to the conclusion
* Transitions cleanly from one point to another
* Have an engaging start
* Have a clear message and/or purpose
* Have a memorable ending
* Be written for allotted time

In addition to this you may also consider

* Creating imagery of any situation. For example, instead of saying "I drove to his house", you could say "I sat in my car, turned the ignition on and started driving to his house"
* Making sure that the story keeps moving forward
* Repeating the core message enough times to ensure message is delivered
* Limiting the number of facts or number of messages to however much an audience can remember. Most of us will remember 1 to 4 points so this may be a decent number
* Adding personal experiences or stories to make presentation more meaningful and trustworthy
* Adding light humor that can be acceptable to the audience
* Using visual aids like pictures, objects, charts or slides to supplement your message
* Including verifiable statistics, true stories, fables and historical facts
* Adding rhetoric questions to underscore key point and keep the audience engaged

What you do not want to do.

* Talk down to your audience
* Take credit of someone else's work
* Write as if you are the ultimate authority of a subject unless you founded a unique idea

Steve Jobs' (CEO of Apple) 2005 Stanford commencement address had many great features of a powerfully written speech. First, Steve told everyone that he had 3 key points to make. By stating that he was going to make only 3 points, he not only gave the impression that his speech will be short and sweat, but also engaged the audience, so they don't miss his limited key points. Secondly, Steve added light humor about Microsoft and his own graduation that never happened. Lastly, he interweaved all his powerful messages with his own personal stories, which made him more relatable.

When writing your speech, carefully consider all key points mentioned above however additionally you could also document how you will change your voice inflections based on content of the speech and where will you add pause or when will you ask a question from audience. All these hints can act as cheat sheet during speech execution.

A properly defined plan for your speech and well written speech shows your discipline and organizational skills, just as sports have certain discipline and organization. In my view, most people are afraid of public speech because they do not do their homework. We are quick to assume that great public speakers walk to the stage and just do it however this is not true for most well-known public speakers, artists and singers. They carefully and thoughtfully plan and practice before they present themselves. Thomas Friedman, a well-known journalist and author once said, "When I was growing up, my parents told me, 'Finish your dinner. People in China and India are starving. 'I tell my daughters, 'Finish your homework. People in India and China are starving for your job.'". If you are not going to do your homework, someone else will do theirs. Good homework will ensure a good speech.

EXERCISE:
Put following plan in order of execution

1. Write your speech
2. Pick a date and location to speak
3. Practice your speech
4. Pick a topic that moves you

LEARNING:
Success in public speaking world is not your first step. If you have a goal or a dream to be good at something than have a realistic and practical plan to show you are serious. You must follow the plan and work hard to get better. Remember, nothing is free in this world, except the love of a mother.

EVERY COMPETITIVE SPORT AND EVERY PUBLIC SPEECH DEMAND METICULOUS PLANNING

Chapter 4

VISIT A DRIVING RANGE

Whether sportspersons visit a driving range to practice golf, spar before a boxing match, knock before a table tennis game, pitch in a bullpen, net practice in cricket or work out to prep their muscles for any sport, they are practicing for a match. In fact, we all practice for every competitive activity in life, whether it's a marathon that we may simply want to finish, our school exams, certification exams or even when we do wedding rehearsals.

Soccer teams tend to play many pre-season and friendly games to prepare themselves while football and basketball teams play scrimmages. Clayton Kershaw may be one of the best pitchers in Major League Baseball, but he practices pitching minutes before he walks into the field. Every other pitcher no matter how famous or ordinary he may be, practices minutes before starting to pitch.

I do not know of any sportsman or a sportswoman who would not practice before any match. We have seen top football teams practicing the day before their Super Bowl match. We have seen great tennis icons like Roger Federer and Rafael Nadal practicing hours before their grand slam finals. Didn't you wonder why Roger Federer had to practice hours before any match he played in year 2007, where he was guaranteed a victory for every tournament he signed up for? Did Rafael Nadal need any practice before any French Open tournament for more than a decade? Did Serena Williams need to practice for most of the grand slams? Despite of their near certain success we all saw them practicing before every match including first round matches where chances of their challenger's win were no less than winning a mega lottery.

Sportspersons practice before any sporting match because they want to

* Practice their muscles for the game
* Prepare their mind to focus
* Adjust their eyes to the ambience
* Fine tune their shots/spins/pitches
* Get better and perfect their game

Boost their confidence They all practice because they know practice makes them perfect. Practice exposes their flaws and allows them to be perfect. They use different tools to practice their game even if the tools have nothing to do with their sport. For example, table tennis players use shadow boxing to improve their quick step movements or they use a table in playback mode to practice their reaction and improve hand eye coordination. Boxers use punch bags to improve their punch speed or do jump ropes to stay on their toes for longer period and have longer reach by springing forward. Tennis players hit the wall, golf players use driving range, baseball and cricket players use a net and so on.

Practice of sports enthusiasts and athletes includes watching videos of themselves and their competitors to see how they can do better. They also listen to music or motivational talks of their choice before walking into a stadium full of spectators. This is all done to prepare themselves for the big match. Think about 100 meters sprint where Usain Bolt of Jamaica set record for 9.58 seconds. He runs both 100 meters and 200 meters that take less than 10 seconds and less than 20 seconds respectively, but he practices all year for those few seconds. Usain Bolt may be only 5 seconds faster than me in 100 meters sprint, but he is not only most famous athlete in the world, he is also worth over 100 million dollars. If I could only improve my speed by 5 seconds, I could be that rich and famous. This is best example of not only raw talent, but also practice that Mr. Bolt must do all year long. This also tells us, how every millisecond is important in his run. He is obviously not running 100 meters one after the other to practice for big moments, instead he spends many more hours daily to condition his body and mind before he sprints. Similar mentality of hard work applies to public speaking as well. Your most important speech could only be 5 or 10 minutes long, but it requires a comprehensive practice and preparation days and maybe months before you deliver the speech. Like Usain Bolt, your speech may not simply require you to keep practicing same speech over and over. You may practice singing and dancing to improve your voice and body language respectively, or you could start telling jokes by impersonating characters. Your sole objective may still be to become the best speaker you can.

In one of my most important speeches, I had couple of lines of poetry for which I practiced independently by reciting not only the verses in my speech, but also other related poems to find some rhythm. Practice may not give you the voice, but it will give you the confidence. This is from a man who would only sing in front of his dear mother or loving wife and not take risk in front of anyone else.

Speaking in public or in front of your senior management can be a daunting task. We can sometimes hide, or we can pass on those needs to speak, but sometimes we absolutely cannot because we must talk to make our case, or we must talk to survive. This is where practicing the talk would allow us to be ready for those needs.

You should practice before your speech or an important presentation because it allows you to

* Prepare your mind to focus
* Practice your speaking muscles
* Adjust your eyes to the ambience
* Fine tune your punch lines
* Check your body language

* Get better and perfect your speech
* Boost your confidence

When comparing practice required for a sports match versus a public speech, we see no difference between them because both need a tremendous amount of practice. This validates our understanding that we are afraid of public speaking because we do not practice. Try going for a match without a practice and you will see where your confidence level is. The same applies to public speaking, the more we practice, the more confidence we gain. Again, the world's top speakers who maybe naturally gifted, do not go without practicing and without preparing for their primetime.

PRACTICE, PRACTICE, PRACTICE

There are many ways to practice for a speech depending on type, place and audience. Here are a few tools that you can use.

* Mirror
  * Mirror, Mirror, on the wall. Yes, a mirror on the wall can be magical. It can be a friend to some good-looking folks among us but for most of us, it really seems to elevate our imperfections. Isn't this what we want anyways? Mirrors really help us show how we come across as speakers and allow us to be our own critic before any major speech or presentation. I would caution to avoid being too

self-critical because It is possible that you put too much focus on one imperfection while the whole execution maybe well above average.

* Family and Friends
    • You may be a superstar or a hot shot outside of home, but at home you are a child, a parent, a spouse, a sibling or a grandparent. This means you will get an earful each time and they may not even tell you all the awesome things you wanted to hear. Family and friends can help you before and after a speech and ideally you would want to hear them before the speech.
    • Clubs like Toastmasters may offer you best places to get the most meaningful feedback from fellow toastmasters, who are also there to improve their own skills
    • Review your speech execution plan with a friend of what you are going to say and how and when you are going to say it to have the most impact. Here I'll caution to use a friend who can provide most insightful input and not your best friend who will only tell you all the good things in your speech. Be open minded and do not direct your friend in any direction until asked.
* Recording
    • Recording really helps you show everything you said and how you said and wanted to say but couldn't say. Don't be afraid of videotaping yourself, you do

not need to record yourself and put it on YouTube yet. It is too early to go viral.

- Its best to record while you are doing a full-dress rehearsal in presence of some friends, club members or on the stage where you will be speaking.

- You can privately send videos to friends who may be across the globe to get their input. Video recording provides a full view of what audience will see.

- You can use your video recording to monitor your body language. I suggest turning off audio and watch your body movements only to see if it is giving the same message you intend to deliver

- You can also make an audio recording of your speech and listen while driving. This will save you time and will help you find many areas where you could do better

* Commute

- It is not illegal to talk to audience of one, at least not yet. Practice your speech while you commute to work or anywhere that takes longer than 5 minutes.

- Commuting to and from work is the best time to be yourself without anyone watching you. This will allow you to learn your speech, allow you to practice your punch lines and fine tune your vocals to keep the presentation interesting for audience.

The importance of practicing cannot be stressed enough for any speech or presentations. Even, US presidents practice their speeches before presenting to larger crowds. President George W Bush and President Obama both did full rehearsals before their respective state of the union address, as well as visiting the stage where they would be speaking.

While you practice for anticipated speeches or presentations, you can even practice for an impromptu meeting or a surprise run into an executive in an elevator. You can do this by preparing yourselves with preset answers. Your responses may answer their question more directly or may even divert the question. This is no different than politicians who sometime have preset answers questions they cannot even answer.

For example, if an executive asks you about your view of a major enterprise project where you are not even a project or program manager but only a contributor. You could simply say, "The team is doing an amazing job and we hope this project will add considerable value to our company". In one sentence, you have shown team spirit and desire for the project and the company to be successful. Or you can also respond like politicians where they will give answers that they have prepared and keep repeating for all their lives. "Washington is broken, and I'll fix it", "No one cares about middle class", "The rich are getting richer" and so on. In your case, you could say, "The project is targeted to be on time and on budget" or "Project manager or leader is doing a great job. ". Remember any answers is better than being completed stumped by an executive question.

Practice in public speaking has no less importance then practicing for sports because public speaking practice requires several tools to practice including feedback from mentors, need to fine tune content and perfect our key points to ensure message is delivered. Jim Rohn said, "Take advantage of every opportunity to practice your communication skills so that when important occasions arise, you will have the gift, the style, the sharpness, the clarity, and the emotions to affect other people" Practicing your speech has a huge additional benefit of memorization because by practicing over and over you end up memorizing content of the speech. Memorization of content enhances your confidence and makes you sound more authentic. This benefit alone is enough to demand practice before you present.

EXERCISE:
Read the following paragraph aloud 10 times
"Michael Jeffrey Jordan aka MJ was an American basketball player. He played 15 seasons in NBA for Chicago Bulls and Washington Wizards. His leaping ability earned him the nicknames of Air Jordan and His Airness."

LEARNING:
Repetition exposes flaws and allows you to improve and memorize your key points. During this exercise, you may decide not to use word "aka" because it is too casual, and some audience

members may not even understand. You will also realize that use of past tense "was" is wrong. MJ is thankfully alive today, so it should be "is" but with an addition of word "former" for American basketball player

During your rehearsal you will also end up memorizing MJ's nick names, number of seasons he played and the teams he played for. This knowledge will manifest itself as your confidence in the subject.

*PRACTICE IMPROVES
EXECUTION, ENHANCES
CONFIDENCE AND
STIFLES THE FEAR
OF FAILING*

Chapter 5

◇◇◇◇

BE A TEAM PLAYER

B e a team player from head to toe. Yes, not only in the spirit of being a team player but dress to show support for the team, pride in the uniform and a unified focus. Every sports team has a dress code that identifies them. Wearing blue, white and black by Argentina team and its fans gives them a sense of pride, unity and confidence. Following a certain dress code at golf course is an undefined etiquette. Wearing your team's jersey for your team's baseball game enhances the atmosphere in baseball field, shows a sense of belonging to a community and supporting the team.

Sports gear is also worn to support the sport being played. Have you ever wondered why swimming divers wear speedos? Well, it is too much detail but simply speaking it allows flexibility and control on your body. Have you also wondered why cyclists wear tight clothing? The answer is aerodynamics. In a competitive sport, every fraction of second matters and every minute of resistance or distraction needs to be addressed. Sportspersons in badminton, tennis, squash, table tennis and many other sports wear wristbands and headbands. Sometimes this is done only to stop their own perspiration, to not roll down to their hands or their foreheads during competitive points.

How and what you wear also matters in the sport you choose to play. Tennis players do not wear pants for a tennis game because it restricts movement of the player while baseball players will not wear shorts because of the many dives involved in their game that could cause them bruises on exposed skin. Even wearing shorts requires a sportsperson to be mindful of the style that is most appropriate for the game being played. Shorts are different for tennis vs shorts for swimming vs shorts for basketball. If I decide to wear swim shorts for tennis game or the other way around, I'll realize quite quickly that I'll become the odd ball myself with no pockets to put an extra ball in my pocket while serving or maybe I'll be wearing shorts that are too short as opposed to other players in the field. Dressing appropriate to the sport is not only a necessity, but also allows you to blend in and keeps your focus on the goal.

Sportspersons wear appropriate sports gear or uniform for following reasons:

* Show team spirit
* Show focus as a team or as an individual

* Support the movement and the needs of the sport
* Motivate themselves

All athletes and gym goers wear active wear because they feel more comfortable and feel more excited to do exercise. Body builders or the lucky ones who have six packs, tend to wear tight muscle shirts. They may wear muscle shirts to show off their hard work, to feel good, to motivate themselves or they may simply want to immediately see fruits of their hard work. Ladies may wear capris and sports bra because they may have toned legs or midriff to show or simply feel good or may feel more motivated while doing their exercise.

Bottom line, sportspersons dress according to the needs of their sport and they do not want to stand out for unrelated reasons and take attention away from their key objective. Let's see how dressing up relates to public speaking.

DRESS FOR SUCCESS

While there is no such uniform for public speaking, dressing for success is critical. You should dress according to the needs of the audience or the dress that supports your speech, even if it requires you to wear shorts or jeans. If you are making a motivational speech at a gym, then wearing a suit may not help you as much as wearing a muscle shirt with shorts.

I was in a speech competition and one guy came wearing jeans and a tight T-shirt that showed tattoos on his left arm. I wondered why this guy would take a chance by wearing a T-Shirt showing his tattoos in a gathering that is more mature than his age and not everyone is on board with idea of tattoos yet. It turns out that speech was about tattoos. The speech was very funny and no matter what he said, our eyes were going towards his tattoos and remained glued to listening his amusing story of what type of tattoo he ended up having and why.

I'm obviously not suggesting that we should wear T-shirts or put on some tattoos, instead you should always consider the recipients of the message and the message you want to leave. For example, if you are going to present at a Muslim or Jewish gathering, it may be very appropriate to cover your head with a cap or kippah. This will show that you have done your homework and it will also show respect you have for their respective religions.

Philosophy is simple, you look good and you feel good. Have you tried wearing 30 dollars jeans and 300 dollars jeans? Do you feel any different? You can even try 300 dollars jeans that is torn from all over the place. You will notice how different you feel by wearing torn jeans. If you are trying torn jeans for the first time, you may be the one who feels on top of the world or you may be the one who finds it highly embarrassing even though it is covering most of your legs. If you are the one feeling embarrassed, then you may not feel the same embarrassment when you are wearing shorts for sports or even speedo for diving in a swimming pool where most of your legs are naked. Case in point, every dress has a place of its own and if not worn in its appropriate setting, the same dress may put you at a very odd place. Try walking on a beach while wearing a suit? Or try wearing speedo to work? You get the point. Your dress plays a big role in defining who you are.

Dressing appropriately to blend in, is dressing for success. If you are properly dressed, you will feel confident. This is true even if you are wearing an expensive underwear that no one is going to see. Why would Victoria Secret be so success-ful? Why would a Calvin Klein or Armani underwear sell for 30 dollars while you can buy another brand's box of 3 for 5 dollars? You simply feel good by wearing a nicer brand and you feel more confident even though no one can see that.

Your dress will ensure that you do not stand out for wrong reasons and if your dress conform to the beliefs of the audience, it will also give you additional support from your audience and an added boost to your confidence.

You should dress appropriately for your speech because

* It shows that you are with the audience and they are your team
* Show that you care, and you came prepared. Shows respect
* Feel confident which is critical for your success
* Keep focus on the message and not on what you are wearing and how you look

As a safe rule, dress conservatively and you will almost never go wrong. Wearing jeans or any other casual clothing can be safely considered a risk for most speaking forums. It is a good idea to do your homework and learn about the audience and any limitations that maybe predefined of what you can wear and what you cannot. Dressing appropriately may not win you any points but it is guaranteed to not lose you any.

"Wearing the correct dress for any occasion is matter of good manners" (Loretta Young). You must always remember, speech is not for the speaker, but for the audience and you must show them your best personality.

Audience is not only your team but your customers and fans as well. Follow appropriate dress code to ensure you respect the audience and stay on message. This is true for sports and it is very much true for public speaking.

EXERCISE:

Do one of the following

1. Wear a swimsuit and go for shopping at a mall
2. Start doing sit ups in your office cubicle while your colleagues are watching you
3. Try football style tackle in a soccer match
4. Wear a green shirt for a match while your whole team is wearing white

LEARNING:

You should always stick with norms identified for any given location, event or type of audience. It's OK to be different for religious, health and moral reasons however in most other cases you are better off being on the side of your team. Be respectful even if you have something different to say. You serve the audience and they are your team, so keep them on your side.

*BE ON THE SIDE OF
YOUR AUDIENCE
AND THEY WILL
WANT YOU TO WIN*

PART TWO

When the moment is right, will you be ready? This is not an advertisement for Viagra (thought I should quickly clarify my statement), it is all about the moments in life that we get, and we find that we are not ready for those moments. The philosophy of being at the right place at the right time fails if one of the two does not happen. It is up to us to put ourselves at the right place each time and some day that right moment may come when we will hit it out of the park and everyone will remember us for that one single home run.

In mid-nineties I sought asylum in Canada which resulted in complete reset of my career where my career dropped from being an electrical engineer in my birth country to a convenience store clerk. I could hardly afford to study because of the cost involved and family obligations, but I always took some courses with one simple hope that one day someone will ask me, hey Iqbal, have you done this course and I'll tell him/her that yes, I have. I went through a 5 years long dark tunnel, but then the day came when I received a call from Silicon Valley and yes, I was ready for that moment. While I still consider this a miracle, it would not have happened, had I not tried and had I not kept hope. It is incumbent on all of us, who dream for success that we keep trying. We may fall many times, but we must always find ways to get up and put ourselves in spots where we'll find that beacon of light. As good sports enthusiasts and athletes, we must never give up and just be ready for the right moment.

This part is all about coming out of the long dark tunnel where you have worked hard to prepare yourself to see the light at the end of tunnel. This is the time to show same stubbornness that you have shown so far. Don't let detractors tell you that you cannot do this after so much effort that you put in to getting here. It is time to enter the ring.

Chapter 6

ENTER THE RING

N ow that you have been going to a gym, you planned for the game, you practiced, you dressed up and you have done all you could, it is time to fight. It does not matter who your opponent is or how strong or fast he/she is. If you are baseball player, it does not matter if it is bottom of 9th inning, the bases are loaded, and everything rests on you, nor does it matter if it is the first match in your pool and all you need are 2 points. You are simply walking into a ring or a field of your sport to execute your plan. You cannot take your focus away from the plan you made and the hours you invested in practicing your plan. The crowd, the weather and the opponent do not matter anymore. You remain only in the moment and you do not think what if I fail and what if I hit the home run or score a winning goal in the last play, nothing comes to your mind except the moment. You just walked into a ring or field and all you see is an opponent, everything else fades away.

Every competitive sportsperson who walks in for his or her turn to play is in the following state

* Warmed up before the game or fight by doing some stretching or sport specific routines
* Determined and highly focused on the game
* Unconnected to size and behavior of the audience, even if it is home game
* Knows importance of the moment, but its only at the back of the mind
* Jubilation of success or agony of failure are not at the top of the mind

When sportspersons are walking to take a position, their focus is at the problem in hand. You may have seen many sportspersons wearing headphones and they are listening to music of their choice or a motivational talk. No matter what they are hearing they intend to tune out all other distractions because nothing else matters. They are not worried about how great the opponent is or what will happen if they take that shot or miss it altogether. They are completely immersed in the moment and have the confidence that they have done everything before that moment. They may also know that they cannot change their destiny by doing something they never planned, practiced or heard of. This is simply the time to execute what they practiced for and own the moment.

Owning a moment in sports is simply a confidence on what you have done before and what you feel you deserve. Same applies to public speaking, when you have done all you could before you decided to take the first step to the stage.

OWN THE STAGE

Walking towards the stage is usually the most stressful time of the speech because you are about to face the audience for the first time. This is where I ask you to think like a sportsperson. It's time to reap benefits of all the training you did. This is the time to visualize success. Your team needs you and the audience needs you to make your best effort. This is the time where you should feel the most confident about what you have already done. If you are dressed appropriately, you will already have won some brownie points with audience and if you can walk and stand with confidence, you have earned some more points. Remember, you have not started talking yet. Take a moment before you say anything and know that your thorough planning has brought you here. You have been going to a club, dressed appropriately, and practiced thoroughly, this is the time to execute the final step of the plan.

Key elements that you should be considering.

* Warm up before reaching the stage
* Focus on the speech you practiced
* The audience only wants to hear what you practiced
* The importance of this moment should only be at the back of your mind
* Do not assume success or failure before you even execute the plan

Remember, a little bit of nervousness is natural. You should feel some butterflies in your stomach as your mind and body is telling you to react with caution. This is where your mind will tell you to execute the plan. I read a story of a woman who had mastered the art of speaking to the extent that she was no longer feeling butterflies, she decided to do acting on stage because she was missing the feeling of butterflies in her stomach. There will be times you will love to have butterflies in your stomach because they act as your check to ensure you will not wing your speech with errors.

By the time you walk to the stage, you have already done all your homework because you are a responsible speaker. Warmup your vocal and body muscles just as you would do for any sport. Flex your body a little, clear your dry throat, try saying a passage or two from your speech or maybe sing a song. The best physical exercise is forcing yourself to smile. This simple exercise will reduce tension from your body and take away all mental stress. Once you are warmed up, walk to the stage as if you own it because your focus is not on the audience or future result of the speech, but confidence in your hard work, practice and planning.

Always know that not everyone will love your speech, it is a fact. We live in a world where some humans see green as blue. Every religious person thinks his/her birth religion is perfect. You can bring Al-Gore to speak about environment, Barack Obama to speak about democratic values, the Pope to talk about peace in the world or Malala Yousafzai to talk about girl's education but, there will always be people who have already made up their mind.

Furthermore, the audience may react to your speech in a completely different manner than you anticipate. One example of this was a presentation I attended about cyber security by David Bay who was Edward Snowden's boss. Snowden is a US citizen who stole sensitive NSA documents and fled to Russia. Everyone in the audience was super engaged because of the speaker's personal pain in the story but there was a moment when the speaker talked about his daughter who wanted to know what happened while he had closed the door and was crying at his wife's shoulders. While telling his story, David became emotional. Some of the audience thought it was funny that the girl was being nosy but, I was lost in the pain the speaker was going through. I heard laughter in the audience and I realized how extreme the emotions were in the hall. Here I am, trying to control my tears while others thought it was funny.

This tells us that you may observe extreme reactions from the crowd. Again, this was all in your practice. Your job is to focus on executing what you practiced, and the audience interprets your speech according to what they think. We'll talk more about how to handle audiences in a next chapter where an eye contact with one person can change your whole perspective about greater audience.

Walking to the podium for your speech is like walking towards the boxing ring, because this is the time when you feel most vulnerable and you feel that everyone is watching every step that you take. It is the time when you must walk with extra confidence, tune out all noise in your head and rely on your preparation. Theodore Roosevelt delivered a speech titled *"Citizenship in a Republic"* which would come to be known as *"The Man in the Arena."* He said, "It is not the critic who counts; not the man who points out how the strong man stumbles, or where the doer of deeds could have done them better. The credit belongs to the man who is actually in the arena, whose face is marred by dust and sweat and blood; who strives valiantly; who errs, who comes short again and again, because there is no effort without error and shortcoming, but who does actually strive to do the deeds; who knows great enthusiasms, the great devotions; who spends himself in a worthy cause; who at the best knows in the end the triumph of high achievement, and who at the worst, if he fails, at least fails while daring greatly, so that his place shall never be with those cold and timid souls who neither know victory nor defeat."

Like sports, this is your moment to shine after all that work you did before the competition. Step in the arena with confidence because you have chosen this to be your sport and you are not playing to lose.

EXERCISE:
Dive into frigid cold water while wearing a speedo or a bikini

LEARNING:
Since the water is cold, you may hesitate to enter and when you do enter, you would want to get in and get out fast. You may also be shivering when you leave the water.

Now try the same thing while wearing a wet suit. You will most definitely not hesitate as much, and you will feel more control on the pace and duration of your exit. You may also not shiver when you leave. Same applies to public speaking, you will walk towards the stage with more confidence when you are prepared for the environment.

*YOU HAVE WORKED
HARD TO ARRIVE
AT THIS MOMENT,
YOU OWE YOURSELF
THE BEST FIGHT*

Chapter 7

BREATHE IN
BREATHE OUT

Proper breathing is a key component of every sport. Sportspersons are taught to inhale, and exhale based on actions they take. Sports are all about rhythms and alignment of movements, muscles and breathing to create the biggest impact. Swimming may stand out to be the number one sport where breath adjustment is most critical and even decisive. Now think about hitting a golf ball. Would you be breathing in or breathing out when your golf club makes contact with the ball?

Let's compare a marathon run with a 100 meters sprint. In a marathon, you will need to pace your breathing for the duration of the run, you may not run too fast early on or in the middle of the run to avoid running out of breath while in 100 meters run you may hold the breath before start of the run but then simply explode and breath adjustment may not be your top priority. In both cases, controlling of breath is critical for runner to complete the run as intended.

Sportspersons breathe in and breathe out in sports

* To relax their body and release muscle tension
* To allow for the moment to set in
* To create an impact

Being able to control breathing can be the difference between an average player and a champion. Novak Djokovic who is one of the greatest players in history of tennis, suffered breathing issues in the beginning of his career which may have ended his career. He mentions in his book, "*Serve to Win*" of how Dr. Igor Cetojevic, a nutritionist and fellow Serb suggested him to change his diet. He realized that Djokovic's breathing difficulties may have been consequence of imbalance in his digestive system which was triggering an accumulation of toxins in his intestines. He tried a gluten free diet for two weeks and we suddenly saw surge of Djokovic's tennis career. He had been world number 1 and a grand slam champion before these problems, but after taking full control of breathing issue, he is now looking to become one of the best in history of tennis.

Inability to control breathing is close to killing a sporting career. Controlling breath is critical to succeed in any sport, and it is no less critical when it comes to public speaking. Let's review how controlling your breath can improve your speaking skills.

CONTROL YOUR BREATH

Thanatophobia is the fear of death where death is a state when we do not breathe. Glossophobia on the other hand, is fear of public speaking where we may forget to breathe. According to several statistics both phobias are in the list of top 10 fears most of us have. Breathing is an antidote to death, we must keep breathing to stay alive, we die if we do not. I guess you learned something new today. Well, the same applies to public speaking, if you hold your breath your speech dies. Breathing is your antidote to relaxing your body and executing your plan the best you can.

Breathing to survive should not be confused with breathing for sports or for public speaking. Breathing for life happens automatically just like our heart that keeps pumping and brain that keeps working to keep our body functional and to keep us sane. Breathing for exercise, sports or public speaking is clearly different because all of this requires you to adjust and fine tune your breathing. You will need more oxygen for bigger impact, so you must inhale before you hit the ball and exhale at the time of impact, so you can send the ball as far as you want it to go. The same applies to public speaking where you will need more oxygen before you project your voice. More oxygen in your body will allow you to control tone, pitch and pace of your speech. Imagine if you were to fast speak a sentence, but you end up running out of breath in the middle of the sentence. Or you wanted to hammer your key point, but your voice failed to support you? This will not only result in loss of confidence for yourself, but your message would not be delivered.

If you do not breathe properly during your speech, it creates the impression that you are nervous. According to experts, this happens because we breathe using our chest versus our bellies to breathe. I found many articles suggesting that we develop habit of breathing using chest as we grow older, while babies breath using their bellies. Breathing through bellies results in full breath while when breathing using our chests do not allow for a complete inhalation. Breathing through chest results in sensation of tightness, causing discomfort and taking our attention away from the audience and the message we want to deliver.

If you can develop a habit of proper breathing (full belly breathes) at all occasions, you may have learned the art of fighting all challenges that life throws at you.

Mastering your breathing has the following benefits.

* Provides oxygen to your brain when it needs the most
* Allows you to make a complete statement at your desired pitch, tone and pace
* Makes you look confident because you take charge of your body and vocals
* Allows for mental focus
* Naturally takes you out from a state of shock and relaxes your body

Our body can go in shock for many reasons and may send messages to our brain to stop the breathing action. You may have seen or heard about situations when a baby cries or experiences a pain he/she may hold his/her breath for a moment. Parents try to blow hard on baby's face to interrupt this breath holding spell. This phenomenon also happens with adults when human body or mind observes a surprise shock. When I heard about my sister's death in Germany, I cried a lot during my whole journey from Los Angeles, USA to Frankfurt, Germany however when I saw her body, my own body and mind went into a shock mode. I had no emotion and I was simply staring at her and thinking if it was real or imaginary. A cousin of mine jolted me from behind and begged me to cry.

Speaking in public is one such scenario where your body feels that it is at a wrong place and it must defend itself in front of so many strangers. This shock can result in changing your breathing pattern which may result in failing to say a single word you wanted to say, or it may not allow you to say how you wanted to say. You may end up mumbling as well.

During a technology conference an anxiety expert asked all of us to control our mind by focusing simply on our breathing and asked us to tell all our wondering thoughts to 'go away'. This exercise was done for more than a minute and every time a thought came, I had to tell the thought to go away so I could focus on my breathing. I quickly realized how relaxed my body and mind felt with such a simple exercise, despite being in a room full of people. Try this for a minute and you will understand the importance of focusing on your breathing.

Taking deep breath before the speech and controlling your breath during the speech requires coordination and training, just like the training done by sportspersons. For example, swimmers spend considerable time practicing their breath alignment with their strokes and time every second they must remain under water to complete a most efficient lap. Similarly, controlled breathing allows you to control your body language. A relaxed body will show fluid movements on the stage and allow for more direct engagement with the crowd. This is an acquired talent requiring you to include this in all aspects of your training before the speech, as discussed in part 1.

Your ability to control your breathing is closely aligned with two other critical components of the speech, pause and vocal variety. We'll discuss value of pausing and vocal variety in next chapters

In this chapter you have learned that breathing is as important in public speaking as it is in sports. While you may not be performing excessive physical exertion in a public speech, your mind and body are feeling same stress and anxiety that you would feel during a physical exercise. Controlled breathing allows you to relax your body, have a mental focus and it allows you to make a bigger impact.

EXERCISE

Try reading following Harry Carpenter's commentary when Muhammad Ali beat George Foreman in 1974

"Suddenly Ali looks very tired indeed, in fact Ali, at times now, looks as though he can barely lift his arms up... Oh, he's got him with a right hand! He's got him! Oh, you can't believe it. And I don't think Foreman's going to get up. He's trying to beat the count. And he's out! OH MY GOD he's won the title back at 32! Muhammad Ali! "

Now take a full belly breath
Read the same commentary again.

LEARNING:

You may run out of breath when you must state long sentences or when you must speak fast to create a momentum or explain a fast-paced event. Taking a breath in the middle may ruin the impact of your statements so you must pace yourself in anticipation. You should take a long breath, if your speech has a long, fast paced sentence or if it requires you to change your pitch significantly. This is where a pause prior to that sentence will allow you to breath and set you up for a clean execution.

ABILITY TO CONTROL YOUR BREATH MAYBE THE DIFFERENCE BETWEEN A PLAYER AND A CHAMPION

Chapter 8

EYE ON THE BALL

You have heard about keeping your eye on the ball. This term is known to have originated in sporting arenas where every sportsperson is expected to keep an eye on the ball. The phrase is known to be recorded for cricket, golf, croquet and baseball while most folks in baseball countries understand this to be originated in baseball field. Regardless of its origin, the idea is to keep your focus on your target.

You will need to keep an eye on the ball in any sport involving a ball. Be it table tennis, tennis, volleyball, baseball, cricket, rugby, soccer, American football, golf or any other sport, you will need to know where the ball is at any given moment.

You keep eye on the ball because

* The ball is the center of everyone's attention
  • Every other element in the sport is only part of your peripheral vision

* The ball must be directed to its target
  * Target maybe between the goal posts, a hole or out of the field
* You need to tune out all distractions
  * Your entire focus must be on the ball and nothing else matters
* You need to avoid getting a black eye
  * You do not want to be hit by the ball coming at you. This maybe a very bad situation for a sportsperson, but it does happen

In sport of boxing or kick boxing, when boxers are called for weigh-in a day before their bout, they not only are weighed but it's an opportunity for boxers to try to stare down their opponent. In other words, they have started boxing with their eyes before they could even use their fists. This shows the power of eye contact in sport of boxing.

If you are running a marathon or doing cross country bicycle race or even if you are doing 100 meters race you will always need to keep an eye on your competition. 100 meters races go so fast that you could miss key moment if you blink, despite of the pace you will see top sprinters keep a very close eye to who they are running against. When Usain Bolt was defending his Olympics title in 100 meters, he ran so fast that he had enough time to look back to his opponents to ensure that he had guaranteed his victory.

Now, let's assume you are playing soccer (football) and you are playing against Lionel Messi's FC Barcelona or Cristiano Ronaldo's Real Madrid and the whole world is watching you with a live audience of thousands staring at you. Would you be star struck? Would you be distracted by noise of the home crowd or booing of the opponent's crowd? Probably not, because your focus will only be on the ball while everything else will be at the back of your mind.

As a sportsperson, you always want to keep your focus on the target, you do not look away from any moves being made by your opponent(s). Initially, you scan your environment and see some spectators who want you to win (your fans) and others who want you to lose. This will happen in every sport you play. Remember, you are always playing for your fans. If you look into their eyes, you will see how much they want you to win.

Imagine you are playing as a batter in baseball. You first acknowledge everything around you, from the fans cheering in the stadium, to the opponents scattered across the field. You then focus on the pitcher who is hungry to get you out, and everything else immediately goes into the back of your mind. Your only mission now is to find every loose ball and hit it out of the park.

Now that you can relate to value of keeping eyes on the ball in sports, let's see how it relates to making an eye contact with your audience.

MAKE EYE CONTACT

While you keep your eye on the ball in sports, making eye contact with your target audience has no less significance because in this case, their eye are your targets. If you are only scanning over the audience, then you are not seeing any single person, but a hall full of seemingly apathetic and lifeless objects, who don't necessarily care about what you are saying. You don't want to see objects but human beings who have a need to relate with you. This can be best done by singling them out, one by one. This stresses the importance of seeing human beings individually.

Here is a simple exercise that emphasizes the importance of visuals accompanied with action. Try standing on one foot, once with your eyes open and once with your eyes closed. You will notice that it is significantly harder to balance on one foot with your eyes closed. This example tells you how quickly you lose control when you cannot see something. You will notice that you can stand on one foot many times longer when your eyes are open versus when your eyes are closed. This tells you how quickly you lose control when you cannot see something. In this example, you don't really need to see anything even if you are standing with your eyes open. This exercise will give you a glimpse into how our mind works when we can see thing versus when we cannot.

Likewise, looking at the audience as a crowd is considerably different from making eye contact with one person. Eye contact allows you to build a personal bond with one person at a time making the delivery of your message more meaningful. I'll call this divide and rule philosophy, where looking at the whole group may intimidate you, but looking at one person at a time changes the nature of your "risk". I think, the fable of 3 bullocks goes very well here. There were 3 bullocks who were always together, and a lion at a distance. The lion's mouth was always watering over such good meal, but he could not eat them because he was afraid of attacking them when they were together. The lion takes help from a fox by promising her security in return. The fox uses her cunning tactics against the bullocks and makes them fight with each other. Now the bullocks were no longer together, and the lion eats them all, one by one. Perhaps this example is a bit graphic, but the moral of the story is clear. If you look at the whole crowd as one, you may find them intimidating, but if you speak with one person at a time, you can deliver your message confidently to not just the one person, but the whole audience.

While you divide and rule, I also advise to not look at one person for so long that the person feels uncomfortable. Make sure you divide this attention among others in the audience. Most people are good hearted, and they will acknowledge your eye contact and give you positive vibes to get you going with your message.

Building a human connection with audience members is key. Once you have that connection you can deliver any message, even if you must deliver bad news. You can even address a hostile audience by first making a connection through their eyes.

You must make eye contact for following reasons.

* To aim at your target
  * Your audience and your message to audience
  * While you focus in one area, everything else must remain in your peripheral vision

* You are the center of attention
  * Your audience wants to make eye contact with you
* Tune out distractions
  * Light, camera, sound system, size and behavior of the audience
* Not get black eye
  * Show the audience you care

Your speech starts before even you reach the stage or podium. Scan the audience and see where they are and how they are acting. Know how the light is directed at the stage and how the sound system works, as well as other specifications such as the height of the podium, and the length of the stage. Once you know all that, you already have control on the peripheral factors.

When on the stage, do not look away from crowd unless you decide to lecture them. Remember, you have fans in the crowd who want you to be successful, find them as soon as you reach the podium. If you do not know anyone in the crowd, find friendly looking people that you can trust. Look into the eyes of any friendly person and make your point by looking at that one fan then move your eyes to another fan, make your second point. Keep repeating this from one fan to another by making sure that you made eye contact. This will ensure that you are not lecturing an adult but having a conversation with one person in the crowd at a time while the whole audience is benefiting from that conversation.

In my personal experience, our company CEO decided to announce a company award during a Christmas party, for presenting the best idea out of 100s of ideas submitted. I knew my idea co-shared with one of my team members was one of the top 3 ideas, but when I found out that we were winners and we had to extemporarily speak in front of an audience of close to a thousand, my amazing team member conveniently told me that she is not going to speak. I quickly thought of all the tools at hand, while walking to the stage, I noticed our Sr. Vice President of Human Resources sitting in the very front seat, and I knew her as a very nice person. I grabbed the microphone, made an eye contact with her, and started speaking. After the first sentence, I had gained enough confidence. I was able to find another friend at the back of the table whom I was sitting with, and I proceeded to finish my second sentence. I came back again to our Sr. Vice President for one last time to finish my thought. A great disaster was averted, thanks to all the hard work I put in at my public speaking club.

Making an eye contact with one or two people takes away the stress of a larger audience. Once you make eye contact, you start talking to one person at a time and the fear of speaking to larger audience will subside.

Opposite of making eye contact would be glancing your eyes over the crowd. Trust me, you will get dizzy and will not be able to deliver your message to the audience. You need to see people with emotions who you can move with your powerful points rather than seemingly lifeless objects. You need people with emotions whom you can move with your powerful points.

Remember, eye contact ensures sincerity and integrity. You will not make eye contact if you are hiding something, so go ahead make an eye contact in every setting and your message will be heard.

Keeping your eyes on the ball is pivotal sports, whether it's a ball or your competitor. You cannot compete if you lose the ball or take your eyes off your competitor. Similarly, in public speaking making an eye contact is critical to connect with audience, and sound more authentic.

EXERCISE
Have a friend sit in front of you. Look straight into the eyes of your friend for one minute and don't blink. Make some mental notes of what you learned about the person.

LEARNING
You may find this funny, friendly, creepy, intimidating or even find it romantic. No matter how you feel, you will at least realize that you have your friend's full attention. You will also learn that you can transmit any message through your eyes without even saying a word.

*EYE CONTACT WITH
ONE AUDIENCE MEMBER
OPENS WINDOW
TO SOULS OF THE
WHOLE AUDIENCE*

Chapter 9

PAUSE AND PLAY

Any tennis player while serving or any baseball pitcher while pitching takes few moments before delivering their best serve. This delay gives the server more control and the receiver more anxiety depending on the state of the game.

Rafael Nadal walks to the serve line, but then he takes time to line himself up to serve, he fixes his shorts, his hair, looks up to his opponent, bounces the ball a few times and then serves. During all this time, he not only thinks about how and where he is going to serve but also prepares himself for each point.

Clayton Kershaw and Max Scherzer are two of the top pitchers in Major League Baseball, if you watch them closely, you will see how long it takes them to pitch each time. This delay can even be longer depending on how critical the moment is. If all bases are loaded, a pitcher must worry about stolen base as well, not to mention he is already under pressure to pitch the best he can.

This controlled delay or pause applies to every sport and thoughtful action taken during the play because it allows sportspersons to be effective. They pause because it

* Allows them to focus
* Allows them to breathe and prepare for next action
* Allows them to read the opponent
* May allow them to control pace of the opponent
* May help agitate the opponent and corner them to make a mistake

No matter how fast a sport is played, players find time to pause before the action. Basketball is one of the fastest games where it takes seconds to go from one side to another. Even then, players take a moment before every shot at the basket. Basketball players take a pause to look back before they slam dunk, even after a turnover has occurred and opponent players are not close enough to challenge them. This is done to ensure they are not surprised by the sudden presence of their opponent in order to guarantee two points for their team.

Now that we have seen value of pause or controlled delay in sporting actions, let's also look at commentators in sports.

Vin Scully is a legendary dodger commentator. He had many famous calls from the commentary box, but his most famous call was, when Sandy Koufax pitched to Harvey Kuenn and Harvey missed the ball, Vin Scully said "Swung on and missed, a perfect game". Scully then said nothing for 38 seconds before resuming his commentary. This very long pause allowed listeners to absorb the historical moment. This pause became one of the most memorable moments of baseball history.

We see such pauses practiced in other sports as well where commentators are silent during last moments or critical points of the game. For example, in tennis, when it is last game of the deciding set where a top ranked player is about to win or lose the match, their fans do not want to hear any predictions or statistics from commentators because they are deeply absorbed in watching the points. The moment itself is telling the story so commentators also avoid drowning the moment with their words.

While focus and taking control of our opponent's move is a key component of competitive sport and a controlled silence adds sensation in sports commentary, it also plays the same role in public speaking where you must control your audience through what you say, how you say and when you say it. Let's review how pause creates impact on your listeners

PAUSE FOR IMPACT

A pause is critical for your message to sink into minds of the listeners. It can be used before the punch line (key message) to prepare the audience for the message and/or after the punch line to let audience absorb your message. As an analogy, our minds work somewhat like our stomachs, we may get heartburn, or choke ourselves by eating too fast. When we are eating, we should allow our stomach to send a message to our brain that it is getting fuller, so we do not keep eating more with no additional benefit. The same applies to speaking

A poem by Judy Brown describes the value of pausing through an analogy of logs. "What makes a fire burn is space between the logs, a breathing space. Too much of a good thing, too many logs, packed in too tight can douse the flames almost as surely as a pail of water would". A short pause or silence is the most powerful tool at our disposal to ignite that fire for both the speaker and the audience. It allows speaker to take a moment to breath, think or show emotion and it allows audience to absorb the message.

I'm not disregarding how silence can be terrifying for the speaker however only the speaker can truly leverage silence to create a meaningful speech. Looking from a different angle it further validates the point that no one knows the importance of momentarily silence than the speaker. If you can take a moment of pause and breathe in presence of large crowds, you may have mastered one of the most powerful tools in public speaking. Pause creates tension and allows speaker to exploit the moment. Mark Twain said, "No word was as effective as a rightly timed pause". Mark Twain used to play with length of pauses depending on the audience he was addressing.

A pause at one part of the speech could be long for one audience but shorter with another. Make the pause work for you, give your audience a moment to catch up with you, a moment to giggle, a moment to shed a tear or a moment to smile. You may have watched interviews on different media where interviewer clearly gives the interviewee a moment to shed tear. If the interviewee sheds a tear, it is the golden moment that the interviewer wanted, and that moment may run multiple news cycles.

A pause or a silent moment during your speech or even during daily conversation has significant benefits because it allows you to:

* Take control and build anticipation at the beginning of speech
* Sound more authentic because you are not rapidly reciting what you practiced
* Collect your thoughts and at times allow your audience to ponder over your point
* Breathe normally and relax your nerves
* Read the audience and pace your speech to the needs of audience
* Transition from one point to another
* Let the message sink into the minds of your audience
* Let audience create the image you are describing
* Let emotions play out
* Let any possible laughter or distraction to subside
* Relinquish control more gracefully at the end of a speech

As a speaker, a pause will not only allow your prior point to sink in to your listener's mind, but also create anticipation for the next. These few precious moments may only be 2 to 4 seconds, but they will allow you to deliver with more confidence. Dov Seidman, the author of "HOW" said "When you press the pause button on a machine it stops. But when you press the pause button on human beings they start",

If you try to go fast your mind maybe left behind, if that happens mind will force feed Ahs and Ums because it cannot find words so quickly. Pause allows you to reflect and it allows, you to think and it allows your audience to absorb. You do not want them to drink through a hose. "And it is not just knowledge that is imposed by pausing, so too is ability to build trust", to form deeper and better connections, not just fast ones with other human beings "adds Dov Seidman

Use the pause, to make eye contact, show emotions and connect with the audience. If you are filling up spaces with "ahs" and "ums" you are basically continuing your speech where the audience is expecting that you are trying to say something, yet nothing is coming out. You may be able to win them back with your next big statement, but by then you may have lost some members of the audience.

Thomas Friedman, the author of the book "*Thank you for being late*" states that his book was sparked by a pause where he had a chance encounter with a stranger in a parking garage. We can clearly see how important it is to slow down in our lives. The emotions conveyed by Mr. Friedman regarding the simple concept of a pause were strong enough to earn the title of a New York Times' best seller.

The act of pausing, allows sportsperson to observe and focus while it gives a speaker a moment to breathe and let the message sink in. A brief silence may seem like eternity, but this is all it takes to leave your message, convey your emotions and let your audience absorb your message.

If I could leave you with one message in this whole book, it would be to think before you speak and give yourself a moment before making any meaningful statement. This idea will even help you in extemporary situations where you did not get a chance to practice or you chose not to train yourself. A moment of pause will show that you thought before you spoke, and in turn shows respect towards the person who asked you the question.

EXERCISE
Tell your closest friend or family member that you have a most amazing and life changing news for them. Then, don't say a word for 30 seconds.

LEARNING:
Pause will enhance the suspense and may create panic for the listener in waiting for what comes next. Use pause wisely, it will allow you to control yourself, your audience and above all the message you want to deliver.

PAUSE OFFERS THE AUDIENCE AN OPPORTUNITY TO ABSORB YOUR MESSAGE AND OFFERS YOU AN OPPORTUNITY TO EXPLOIT THE MOMENT

Chapter 10

BEND IT LIKE BECKHAM

Whether you *Bend it like Beckham* (British Film 2002) or hit a forehand winner like Federer, you will need to use your body positioning and movement to put pressure on the opponent before the ball even touches your racket, bat or a body part. A soccer player who is going to pass the ball to another team member will not speak out to say he/she is going to pass a ball or where the ball is being placed. It would simply be angling of torso or pacing of steps. Baseball pitcher is known for chin gestures and volleyball players are known for using hand gestures behind their back.

In an individual game like tennis, player is not going to hint the opponent about the next serve. In fact, the server will try to trick the opponent to a different direction. Tennis player on the receiving side is trying to do the same, though the receiver does not have the ball. Receiver moves his/her body in such a way that the server feels pressured to rethink multiple times until the server's racket makes a contact with the ball. These small gestures make the biggest impression and can mean the difference between success and failure.

Now let's look at the more dominant players versus other players, we'll notice that the dominant players make themselves look bigger by standing tall or by keeping head high or puffing out chest. All these actions can be natural or unnatural, but they show confidence.

Why is body language important in sports?

* Signals to our team members or opponents for next move
* Shows confidence or position of strength
* Shows current or future positioning of body

When you go hiking, you see signs where you are informed about how to show yourselves bigger if you see a mountain lion. You are asked to raise your hands high, stand tall in your place and if you have a child with you, you should carry the child on your shoulder, so you can look even bigger. This action helps you look stronger to a predator like mountain lion. On the contrary if you try to run or show your back to the lion, you have most definitely invited trouble for yourself because it is a sign of weakness. This is all innate to human beings and animal kingdom.

Controlling your body languages is critical for your sporting activity and so it is for public speaking as well. If your body can deliver messages to wild animals and pets, then it most definitely delivers messages to all human beings. Let's see how you can control your body to send the right messages.

CONTROL BODY LANGUAGE

First of all, you must understand that your body chats even though you may not have uttered a single word. Your body language may even give a message contrary to what you want to deliver verbally, or it may even give out message before you wanted to deliver one. Knowing the value of body language and learning to align the messages is a critical success factor in public speaking.

How is body language important in public speaking?

* Exudes confidence
* Helps in delivering the message
* Shows the audience that you mean what you are saying

Tommy Edison, who's been blind since birth was talking about body language and he said, "While I do not pick up on body language per se, there are other cues that people give off when I talk to them. For example, if someone's joyous, right? Someone is excited, you can hear it in their voice. There's a big smile when they talk. Information is just sort of flowing out of them. They are excited. I just can hear it all in their voice. It is so clear to me. Now, if someone is sad, their voice is going to be a little bit more down, right? They're not going to smile when they talk anymore. Their voice might even quiver, you know. They might sigh a little bit". On one hand this example stresses on the value of vocal variety which we will discuss in next chapter, but on the other hand it underscores the importance of all body gestures including your smile, frown, laughter or bodily excitement and how this effect the words that flow out of your mouth.

When you are interviewing for jobs, in most cases, the very first interview is a phone interview where hiring manager or the recruiter cannot see you. In this case, you are always given advise to make sure that you are sitting up straight during the interview, turn off all possible distractions from the room so you may not accidently start watching the basketball game or start looking outside of window and above all, you are asked to smile as often as you can because your pleasant personality will flow through to recruiter on the other side of the phone.

Smiling during or before your interview or speech can also boost your confidence and reduce stress because smiling relaxes facial muscles and calms the nervous system. According to NeuroNation "When a smile flashes across your face; dopamine, endorphins and serotonin are all released into your bloodstream, making not only your body relax, but also work to lower your heart rate and blood pressure. Endorphins are natural painkillers - 100% naturally produced by your own body, without the negative effects of medication. When you smile, people treat you differently. You're seen as attractive, reliable, relaxed and sincere". Isn't this what you need, when you speak to any audience? Of course, I'm not suggesting that you smile when reading a eulogy because the situation may not ask for any type of humor or light moment however even the most serious messages can have some light moments where you could smile. Remember, smile is contagious which means you can quite easily bring audience on your side by smiling with them.

While smiling is one of many body gestures that you must control, here are some do's and don'ts of body language

Do's
* Stand or sit tall and open your chest
* Face the audience and always keep eye contact
* Move with purpose
* Keep hands to the side except when they need to convey a message
* Smile or show facial emotions for a touching moment

Don'ts

* Putting hands in the pockets
* Hand clasping or crossing of the arms or legs
* Looking down or away from the audience
* Walking back and forth or swaying side to side without any purpose
* Purposeless movement of hands and arms
* Holding podium or lectern at any time during speech
* Drinking, eating or chewing gums
* Winking of eyes

* Standing or sitting inappositely
* Stare at anyone in the audience
* Crouching of body while standing or sitting
* Pointing fingers at anyone in the audience
* Tapping fingers on the podium or lectern
* Tilting or wobbling of head

You may open your arms if you are welcoming someone in speech, put hand on your heart to show love or make a V with fingers to show peace or victory. All hand or body signals should be with a purpose and mindful to the culture of community, city or state. Most of these do's and don'ts apply to a job interview as well with the exception of keeping your hands on the side while you are sitting across the table for an interview. It is usually a good idea to keep hands visible to your interviewer with palms facing outwards

Dr. Albert Mehrabian, the author of Silent Messages, conducted several studies on nonverbal communication. He found that 7% of any message is conveyed through words, 38% through certain vocal elements, and 55% through nonverbal elements (facial expressions, gestures, posture, etc.). of our communication in our meetings, interviews and our speeches. This rule is also known as 7-38-55 rule and it shows how body language dominates nonverbal portion of our communication

While you may be afraid to utter words from your mouths, you just learned that you will need to train your body to speak. You do not want your body to send a message that you did not intend to deliver verbally. For example, when you ask your child, to say sorry to the other child. The child may quickly utter the words "I am sorry" but then you may ask the child to repeat the same words and this time, really mean those words. This is because the child did not show remorse which was critical for message to be trustworthy.

In earlier chapter, we talked about butterflies in our stomach and how there is a benefit to having butterflies because many time butterflies will act as a check on your body, so you don't keep rambling everything that comes to your mind. When you understand the needs of the audience or happiness or a sadness of a person, you will be able to deliver your message most effectively. As an example, let's assume an under-privileged person tells you about winning a lottery of 1000 dollars which may not be an amount for you to be excited about, but it may be a life changing amount for the other person. In this example when you understand the circumstances you may be able to show more excitement and express yourself in better words instead of thinking from your angle where a thousand dollars does not change anything for you. You could say "good for you" versus "wow, I am so happy for you". You could also stay still and ignore the person's excitement versus open your eyes wide and show a big smile.

Your body language and your choice of spoken words will always complement each other. Alignment of your body language with your spoken words adds a boost to your message. On the other hand, your body may give a different message than the one you intend to deliver. You may also choose to stay quiet, but your body may not. Make your body support your message.

Body movements and body signals are integral part of every sport. Just like a sportsperson who must control body language, a public speaker must control body signals being sent. Audience will get confused if your body is sending a different message then what you are verbally delivering. This makes it important for you to understand value of body language and work to align your body to the message you intend to deliver verbally.

EXERCISE:

Assume someone shared a great news with you and you are responding to the person's excitement.

Say "Wow, I am so happy for you" but say it without a smile, without opening your eyes wide and without moving any part of your body.

Now think about how you felt when making this simple statement. You must have felt that the word "wow" cannot be said without prolonging of the word and without expressing extreme excitement or even extreme disappointment.

LEARNING:

We are humans, not robots. We have feelings that we express through our body parts. During your speech try to express your feeling through your body gestures that are well aligned with your message. You will not sound authentic if you don't feel what you are saying. This is true even when you are on the phone with someone.

YOUR BODY NEEDS TRAINING TO SPEAK WHEN YOU WANT IT TO SPEAK AND STAY QUIET WHEN YOU WANT IT TO STAY QUIET

Chapter 11

G-O-A-L

After you bend it like Beckham, you will still need to manage pace and spin of your kick. Your delivery to the goalkeeper or the recipient of your shot is total sum of your body positioning and variety in the delivery. You will need to be unpredictable and you will need to keep your opponent guessing. You cannot score a goal in soccer or a touchdown in American football by running in a straight line. Take table tennis as an example, if you serve the opponent with the same pace, length, height, spin and at the same place, the opponent will not let you win points, unless the opponent is new to the game. Even in that case, wouldn't you feel mercy on the player and serve it easier, so he/she can return? Same applies to public speaking as well, you cannot continue to pace yourselves at the same tone, intensity and frequency.

A sportsperson cannot play the same style of game with different opponents. Game with every opponent must be planned differently while some tweaking to the game maybe required during the match. This allows for exploiting weaknesses of opponent.

Sportspersons modify their game execution because they want to

* Find weaknesses in the opponent by trying different spins and different game styles
* Keep them guessing and direct them in making mistakes of judgement
* Keep challenging their engagement and keep building pressure
* Test out physical movement or to understand their game plan
* Adjust with the conditions of the play

Rafael Nadal is one of the greatest players in history of Tennis. One of his unforgettable matches was in the semifinals of 2008 Australian Open, where he lost to Jo-Wilfred Tsonga, a French player. This is a game where Nadal found himself completely outclassed by a player against whom he still has more than twice the winning record. This happened because of how Tsonga changed the pace of his game and came to the net so often that it completely got Nadal off guard. This maybe an extraordinary situation for Nadal however this happens a lot in every sport where the player must change pace of the game to stay competitive and win key points.

In team sports like field hockey or soccer, players call other players to tell them of where to pass the ball and sometimes they tell them if they are open. You can see how tone and pitch of their voice changes depending on the criticality of the moment. They might say "over here" or "OVER HEAR". They may say, "I'm open" to indicate their availability or "I'm opennn" by prolonging the word "open", which shows frustration when someone didn't pass the ball while the player was open. These examples tell us that, it's not what you say, it's how you say it, matters. Now, let's look at sports commentary as an example, Andres Cantor's shout of "Goooooaaaaaalllll" is one of the most famous shout outs of team scoring goal. How a simple announcement of a team scoring a goal becomes the most exciting moment for the fans of the team scoring the goal and how it sinks hearts of the fans for the other team. This simple prolonging of the word "goal" by Andres made him one of the most sensational commentators in the soccer world.

When properly timed, your vocal variety may make you famous one day. Now, let's compare variety in sporting actions and execution, with value of showing vocal variety in public speaking.

SHOW VOCAL VARIETY

Dr. Albert Mehrabian's theory of 7-38-55 shows, how vocal variety is the second most important element in conveying of a message. With 38% of our message conveyed because of our vocal variety, his study concludes that 93% of our communication has nothing to do with what we say. It's all about how we say it using our body as a tool, followed by our vocals.

It goes without saying that a monotonous speech will not create any excitement for the audience because it would be clearly missing 38% of communication which directly relates to tone of the voice. A toneless speech has a high probability of being forgotten or being taken as credible. Speeches and presentations that employ vocal variety will leave the strongest impression.

Vocal variety has following benefits:

* Allows speaker to control emotions through inflections of voice
* Allows speaker to control rhythm of speech
* Keeps the audience engaged
* Shows you are prepared and you care for their time
* Keeps the audience guessing of what you are going to say next and how you will say it

Every time you change the pitch and tone of our speech, you are trying to send a message. When I was growing up, my dear dad would call me by my first name, but sometimes the same call was with a raised pitch and it meant something completely different. The tone of my father's voice would give away his intended message and it mostly meant that I must come up with some good excuse or run to my mother for support or hide behind her as my ultimate defense.

In your speeches, you can give very different messages with the same word or same sentence by saying it in a different way. One of my speeches was titled "What difference does it make" and I used this line a few times in my speech, but when

I used this for the first time after building some emotion in my crowd, I said "What DIFFERENCE does it make" showing anger on discriminating human beings based on their race, religion, color, gender or sexual orientation, but when I ended the speech with same words, I had an extremely mellow tone showing the tiredness in my voice and my voice fading away because I wanted to leave the podium with a message of why would you discriminate someone based on human characteristics that they did not choose.

I cannot forget a speaker who was training us on management techniques. He was teaching us about never assuming about an employee, if the employee was not performing or coming in late to work. He suggested that we should always sit with employee and try to find out and see if he/she needs help instead of trying to correct their behavior by force. I never forgot this lesson because of the story he shared. He told us a story of fisherman and the empty boat. Fisherman's boat was anchored, and he was fishing meanwhile an empty boat started drifting towards him and it was most definitely going to collide with fisherman's boat. Fisher man gets angry, so he screams at the top of his lungs, "HEY YOU FOOL, CAN'T YOU SEE, YOUR BOAT IS ABOUT TO HIT MY BOAT". When the boat came closer, not only he realized that boat was drifting away from home, but it was empty. The lesson of the story was that we should not assume about our employees until we sit and talk with them and understand their situation. I heard this story several years ago, but I didn't forget the moment when speaker screamed like the fisherman in the story and paused to let his emotions sink in. When he screamed, it felt as if this had just happened, there was pin drop silence in the audience of about fifty people and he totally took control of his presentation and got undivided attention for the rest of his presentation. That day, not only I learnt a valuable management lesson, but learnt how to keep the story authentic and meaningful for the audience.

Speech should not be about wondering around with no purpose, but you must go with destination in mind and your destination is the message you want to leave. Leave the message with conviction, show emotions in your voice and do not forget to let it sink with the audience. A very short pause along with emotions will give you control on the audience and help you leave the message.

Here are some do's and don'ts for vocal variety.

Do's
* Hydrate before and during presentation, if needed
* Warm up your voice before a speech
* Change pitch, tone and pace
* Breathe to allow your lungs to support key moments of vocal changes
* Show vocal emotions and plan how you will compose in case emotions run too high

Don'ts

* Drink coffee or soda which could dry your throat
* Smoke just before the speech

* Read with single tone
* Speak too fast or too slow
* Whisper that cannot be heard
* Scream too loud or scream without building up anticipation
* Expect from microphone to help you in your vocal variety
* Clear your throat
* A monotonous speech lacks variety making it lifeless and easily forgettable. Vocal variety adds life to your speech because it helps you add emotions, engage audience and make you sound more relatable

Like sports where you must keep changing your tactics to keep challenging your opponent, in public speaking your vocal variety allows for tempo of speech to change and keep audience engaged for the length of speech. It also makes the speech more dynamic and appealing to the audience.

EXERCISE
Scream at the top of your lungs. Caution: Close all doors and warn your family members or roommates before hand

LEARNING:
You may learn something new about yourself or realize what you can do with your voice. Short of vacating your

neighborhood without even saying a single word, you realize how controlling pitch and tone of your voice can send different messages

Your voice has power, show fluctuations and align tone and pitch of your voice with your message.

CHANGE OF PACE SEPARATES A GOOD SPEAKER FROM AN AVERAGE

Chapter 12

LAST PLAY

N ow that you have scored the goal and learned some good tools and techniques about public speaking. In this process, you also learned how those tools and techniques closely relate to the sports.

Before we close, let's revisit argument of whether public speaking is a sport or not. For sportspersons among us, let's ask a question, is golf a sport? There have been many arguments that golf is not a sport because there is no significant physical exertion involved. I'm not going to contest this argument, but I'll say this, in a court of public opinion, it is a sport. For now, let's stick to our epilogue and see if public speaking is a sport.?

Let's look at definition of sports from oxford dictionary

Formal definition of sport:

"An activity involving physical exertion and skill in which an individual or team competes against another or others for entertainment". Example: I used to play a lot of sport or I won 200 meters in school sports

Informal definition of sport:

"A person who behaves in a good or specified way in response to teasing, defeat or a similarly trying situation". Examples: go on be a good sport or John is a bad sport

Formal definition of public speaking

"The action or practice of addressing public gatherings; the making of speeches"

After reading the book and looking at the definitions, I guess, by now you know the answer to the question "Is Public Speaking a Sport?". For your reading pleasure and comparison, let's look at these commonalities and differences between sports and public speaking

Public speaking does NOT include following key elements of sports.

* Cardio
* Physical strength
* Profound sweating
* Breathing hard
* Tiredness

Public speaking includes following key elements of sports.

* Training at the Gym – Public speaking club
* Coaching –Mentoring
* Planning of the game – Doing homework and writing with purpose

* Practicing before the game – Practicing before a public speech
* Wearing the sports gear – Dressing for success
* Unfreezing of your body – Controlling of body language
* Keeping eye on the ball – Making an eye contact
* Taking a moment before the serve/pitch – Pausing to transition and shift focus
* Controlling of your breathing – Breathing during presentation
* Variety of serve/pitch – Vocal variety
* Win or Lose – Successful or Unsuccessful presentation
* Never Quit – Keep presenting

It is important to note that first 6 key points take place before you even stepped in front of a podium. The idea of this book is not to define a new sport or to manipulate the definition of sports as we know it. Instead the idea is to help find that competitive spirit deep within you and challenge you to speak just as you do for any sport, game or activity you truly enjoy doing.

THE RESULT:

Public speaking is not a sport to stay physically fit, however for you to be successful in a culture where the onus is on speaker and not the listener, you should be a good sport and learn to speak in front of teams, strangers, executives or community settings to progress in your careers and to make a difference.

EXERCISE

Do one of the following for two minutes.

1. Run as fast as you can
2. Do as many jump ropes as you can
3. Hold yourself at a plank position
4. Read a book loud at the top of your lungs

LEARNING:

Reading loud may give you same tiredness as you would feel for any of the other physical activity. Now ask yourself, can you improve your stamina and execution with better planning, practice and improved training?

Public speaking may or may not be a sport. This argument may be a moot point when you agree that the fear of public speaking can be muted by following similar strategy as sports.

I rest my case!!!!

Well my friends, this was my last pitch and the end of second half. Best of luck and I hope I made a difference in your life!!!!

LIFE IS A SPORT
AND YOU MUST
TRAIN YOURSELVES
TO RESPOND TO
EVERY CURVEBALL IT
THROWS AT YOU

PART THREE

Public speaking offers challenge, excitement and an inherent need for you to be successful in your professional lives. Your ability to speak better also addresses your need to be heard and understood in your social lives. While sports offer challenge, excitement and many social and health benefits, your need to be more articulate addresses your fundamental need to stay relevant and live a meaningful and more impactful life. This part talks about top qualities of a public speaker, top takeaways and examples of some of my speeches.

Chapter 13

TOP 5 QUALITIES

While sports are an entertainment for sports enthusiast, public speaking is entertainment and an opportunity for education to those who listen. Here are top 5 qualities of a sportsperson and a good public speaker

1. Plays to win
   You never lose hope and keep fighting until you win. You must remain competitive and never give up. In sports, you could be a few points behind and the game is about to end, but you fight to win until it's over. A good speaker may have made some comments or jokes that may not have sat well, but the speaker fine tunes execution as he/she proceeds with the speech.

   When you play to win your audience may think you are overconfident. Although you may want to adjust your execution, it's better to be overconfident than being afraid. Your confidence allows you to control your actions.

Self-doubts are checked at the door because focus is on execution to the plan and adapting quickly to changing circumstances is critical to win.

You celebrate success however you are always humble and always give full credit to the effort made by others.

2. Team player

A good player will never blame the team or circumstances of the play for failure and he/she will always credit the team for success. Sportsperson is expected to play in all weather and field conditions and if he/she blames those conditions, it will only make him/her a sore loser and it will not help in any improvements.

A good speaker is expected to mitigate all risks to execute speech as best as he/she can and if something fails during the speech, he/she will never blame the host or audience or circumstances. You win as a team, you lose as a team.

3. Respects authority

A good sportsperson will almost never question a referee and a good speaker will never question the audience. You can never win by blaming others for your failure. This point again stresses on staying positive to succeed. Positivity boosts confidence and confidence is everything.

4. Committed and determined

   A good sportsperson and a good speaker remain focused to task at hand and tune out all other distractions. You may lose a point, a game, a set, a match or a championship, but you come back at it stronger. You must have high tolerance for pain to be successful. Failures do happen to the best in the world as well, but they show more determination and more commitment than most of us to reach pinnacles of their fields.

5. Evaluates failure

   You win some, you lose some, but a good competitor learns from failures, shows grace in failure and perfects before next attempt. Players like Kobe Bryant in basketball, Alex Rodrigues in baseball and Tiger Woods in golf have lost many a times, but they are still known to be greatest in their respective sports because they review what went wrong and find another gear next time around. Top radio hosts, TV journalists and public speakers have fallen flat when they made big mistakes because of their overconfidence however they all dust off their failures to rise again after learning from their mistakes

Chapter 14

TOP 3 TAKEAWAYS

I'm choosing following 3 key takeaways that can be your life-savers even if you choose not to train, practice or do anything to become a good public speaker. I'll call it 1,2,3 punch. This 1,2,3 punch will apply to every extemporary situation in life.

1. Eye contact
   - Eyes are window to a human soul – Puts us on par with everyone else
   - Allows for conversation – Takes stress of public speech away
2. Pause
   - Allows to think before you speak – It is very respectful
   - Helps convey and control emotions – Leaves lasting impressions

- Provides time to breathe – Keeps us operating in normal mode

3. Breathe
    - Releases body tension – Allows for better body messaging
    - Relaxes vocal muscles – Easier to speak and control our pace, pitch and tone

I believe these 3 techniques are foundational to everything else. If you can master 1,2,3 punch, you will take away all your fears of public speaking.

By making eye contact, you have decided to confront your threat instead of running away from it and by picking one person at a time you have quantified your threat instead of generalizing the threat that everyone is out there to get you. There is a question asked for problem solving, how do you eat an elephant? The answer is, one bite at a time because you cannot eat the whole elephant at once. It's the same as divide and rule. You make eye contact with one person at a time and you end up tacking the whole crowd.

By pausing during your talk, you show control on yourself and your audience. Now, you can control their emotions and make them laugh, cry or think. These emotions engage them with you and they become your partners.

By breathing during your talk or during your pause, you take your body out of the shock that it may have experienced. Now, you can express more with your body language, you can control your pace, tone and pitch of your voice. If your body is tense, you cannot move it at will and your efficiency will decrease considerably. Normal breathing will make you look normal and more confident.

1,2,3 punch can also help you in situations where you find yourself completely speechless. For example, if someone asks you to answer these types of questions in front of an audience of 5 or more people.

* Your boss just told you that you are being laid off. How would you react?
* Let's assume you are a football and you will be used in the Superbowl. What is going through your mind?
* You are being confronted by your spouse who just found out a dirty secret that you have been keeping. How would you respond?

These are either fictitious questions, extremely painful or most embarrassing situations. It may be very difficult to answer this kind of question, so think 1,2,3 punch. Pause, find a friendly person to look at and breathe normally. Breathing normal will allow your body to relax and allow you to make some body gestures including smile at this question and try to be a good sport. You may end up not saying much to answer, but you may have earned some brownie points by thinking, making eye contact and breathing (staying relaxed), as a result showing your confident self.

Chapter 15

SPEECH EXAMPLES

These speech examples provide suggestions of how you can write, practice, memorize and execute to leave biggest impact. These examples have italics text in parenthesis as suggestions which you could very well write in your own speech and take it with you to the stage or simply use it during practice.

I prefer to start each speech by making a strong visual contact and a big smile because visual contact allows me to bring everyone's focus to me and the smile allows my body to relax.

WHAT DIFFERENCE DOES IT MAKE?
SPEECH INTRODUCTION:

This is a speech where I won club and area contests. Story in this speech moves from one country to another and ends at yet another country. This shows movement of the story, but it starts with creating a visual imagery of a situation. This story brings a country to life by comparing her with a mother who can express her feelings. Story has light humor to show that this is not about anger instead it is about emotions and it is about doing the right thing for our country.

SPEECH BEGINS:

It was a beautiful summer night, 11:30 PM, my telephone rings. *[pause to let audience visualize]* On the other side of the phone is a very friendly voice. It was my mother, it was my country of birth, it was my motherland *[hand over heart to show love]* who gave me birth. She tells me that I must run as fast as I can and hide as quickly as I could. She told me that she will always pray for me, she told me that she will always love me.

I hung up the phone. I begged and cried *[show facial emotion]* to the citizens of my country who were my family member, but they all told me that they do not want me in their family. They told me that I was different. *[pause to digest the pain in story]*

I looked at my mother *[eye contact with a different person to hammer this point]*, she was standing silent, helpless, crying profusely. She was heard saying to herself, Tonight, I'm going to lose yet another son of mine. *[pause because this moment needs to be understood]*

I had a choice to make. Choose "Life with Hope" Or hope for even having a life. I chose "Life with hope"

Overnight, I found myself in Montreal, Canada where I was adopted by my new mother who welcomed me with open arms. *[open both arms to show warm welcome]* She told me that she will always love me. She told me that she will always fight for me and she told me that I'll never be different in her family. *[pause and show gratefulness]*

My new family members were so loving that they would always tell me "You first" and if I responded by saying "No, you first", they did not want to be outdone, they would respond with even further zeal, "No, no you first". *(pause to give a moment to smile)* And in their very friendly Canadian accent they would tell me, "You are our family member eh" *[pause to give a moment to smile for audience and for me to plan for next part of the speech]*

My new loving mother gave me so much love and she treated me like her natural born son, but she could not give me opportunities that I deserved so one day she told me that "I must fly as high as I can *[raise head to the sky]* and go as far as I could". She told me that she will always love me, she told me that she will always fight for me and she told me that I could always run back to her waiting arms if I ever needed her. *(pause to allow imagining love of a mother)*. With that love in my heart and the desire to succeed in life I was adopted by yet another mother.

My newest mother was as loving as my two other mothers, she not only gave me love and equality, but she also offered me opportunities that I never had before. *[speak in poetic style]* I started to dream like a child again. *[pause]*

9/11 happens. My mother was deeply wounded, she was hurt *[show bodily pain]*, she was on her knees. Seeing her weakness some of my family members, screamed at her.

MOTHER, why adopt this child from a different country,
MOTHER, why adopt this child from a different religion
MOTHER, why browning of our family *[lower tone of voice to show how bad it is getting]. [pause to let audience absorb sensitivity of the time and how some of our fellow citizens were trying to exploit a weak situation, not understanding that this was the time to unite]*

When my mother heard this, she was deeply hurt, she got angry, she found courage, she stood up and responded to those detractors with extreme anguish. *[show anguish]*

WHAT DIFFERENCE DOES IT MAKE? If my child was born in United States, Mexico or Pakistan
WHAT DIFFERENCE DOES IT MAKE? Whether my child is Jewish, Hindu, Christian or Muslim
WHAT DIFFERENCE DOES IT MAKE? Whether my child is black, white or brown.

I'm United States *[pause]* and I'm the best mother of all. *[pause to allow audience to understand how a mother responded with full determination]*

My friends,

United States is a country which adopted a son, who grows up to become Albert Einstein *[pause]*

This is a country which gave birth to an African American son of an immigrant, a middle-class child, who grows up to become the most powerful man in the world. *[pause]*

United States is envy of many nations. This unconditional love of United States has made it the greatest country on this planet earth. *[pause]* And we must work hard every day to keep it as great as it always was.

[fast pace statement without conjunctions to show continuity]
We do not choose to be born in a certain country, we do not choose to be born in a certain religion, we do not choose color of our skin or gender or sexual orientation.

But we do choose to be, who we are as people and we must make right choices.

[Pause before closing and hammering on key point]

* *"mein amrica ka shehri hoon" [long pause to make audience expect more because this is clearly a foreign language]*
* *Soy un ciudadano de estados Unidos [short pause because this language is somewhat understandable]*
* I'm a citizen of United States

WHAT DIFFERENCE DOES IT MAKE if I speak Urdu, Spanish or English?

WHAT DIFFERENCE DOES IT MAKE if I'm citizen by birth or by adoption? [long pause]

[lower tone as you complete this last statement] What difference does it make? *[short pause and then look at the host to handover control]*

LET REJECTION STING
SPEECH INTRODUCTION:
This is a speech where I'm not only trying to engage the audience with questions but motivate them at a time of rejection. This required me to have many pauses to engage audience,

show vocal variety and body gestures to express grief that we would feel upon any rejection.

SPEECH BEGINS:

Question 1:

How many of you have been rejected by someone at any point in your life? *[raise your own hand and wait for audience to raise their hands. Keep asking leading questions]*. Rejected at a job interview? *[inquisitive facial expression and hand gesture]* Rejected by your lover? *[inquisitive smile]* or rejected by society?

If it is any consolation just know that you are not alone in rejection. If it is any consolation than know that rejection hurts every human being. It hurts to the **core** of our bodies. *[bring both hands to your stomach and express pain in your body through vocals]*

Question 2:

Are there times when you feel that you are NOT getting the deal that everyone else is getting? You pray and work so hard, but you still do not get what someone else got?

Let's look at this for a minute, do you think life would function if all of us got that amazing deal?

What if we all win a mega jackpot each? Would we all be here? Would this club exist? *[smile]* Would I be going through the torture of making this presentation in front of you *[smile, maybe giggle, pause and give them time to laugh. Remember how you say it, makes all the difference]*

We are here because we must respond, we are here because we must fight to earn our rights. *[pause]*. Prayers or desires alone will not fulfill our needs.

Sometimes we pray, and hope God will solve all our problem as we wish. We ask God, please, please, please. However, there are times when we feel rejected by none other than the God Himself. *[put some weight on "Himself"]*

Doesn't this happen to all of us at some point in our lives? *(pause to let it sink and prepare for the joke)*

One man needed something, and he started praying to God.

Man: Hey God – How long are 1000 years
for you?
God: It is only a minute
Man: How much is a million dollars for you?
God: Its just 1 penny.

Man thinks he has God cornered and asks: Hey God, can I have one penny please?

God would not be cornered, and He responds: Wait a minute *[smile]*

(pause to allow for humor to set in and joke to subside)

[get serious] It hurts, it hurts to core of our beliefs. This is the time to understand how practical it is for God to give every one of us what we want.

Would this life function if all of us had a million dollar?

Would this life function if we were all executives or Vice Presidents of a company?

Would this life function if we were all equally intelligent or equally healthy? *[pause]*

There are times in life when we feel entitled to success. We feel that we have everything needed for success and we check all the boxes. Remember, we as human beings do not even have entitlement to life itself *[pause]*. We fail or fail in life because of our intelligence and our hard work or lack thereof. *[long pause before getting to the point]*

[make eye contact with one person to deliver the message] There are times you will not feel lucky, there will be time when you will feel rejected however I ask you today to start looking at less fortunate, it may very well change your life.

If it is any consolation, there are millions of people in United States who sleep hungry. There are millions who are dying of incurable diseases. *[pause and prepare for a real story]*

After being rejected at my own interview for a very nice job where I thought I exceeded their requirements, I was feeling the sting. I went to the gym and I was sitting at the gym waiting for my class to start. I saw a man standing next to me who was over 6 feet tall, over 250 pounds, had big biceps probably bigger than my thighs, in short, he was a very intimidating figure. I was sitting there and thinking of my own rejection that day and at that point I overhead him talk about taking it easy on his exercise that day. Instructor asked him if everything was ok and he responded by saying, one of his kidneys was acting up. I almost cried and thought to myself that here

I was thinking about a rejection of an interview and here is a well-built guy fighting a serious health issue. *[make eye contact with one person]* All that glitters, is NOT gold, put your pain in a bigger perspective *[pause]*

Next time you go to Laguna Beach and look up to multi-million-dollar beach front houses, keep in mind that the house maybe great, but the person inside maybe fighting custody of his children, she might simply have a heart burn where she cannot even eat the amazing food or even have good wine.

[Make eye contact with another person] I know it is harsh to look at people in more misery than yourself however if you do look down for a few seconds, you may not feel rejected. *[pause]*

If you are rejected, it must be for a reason. Let it sting, because it is supposed to sting. Maybe it's there to humble you. Maybe it's there to make you better. *[pause]*

[Find a different person to look at] We must respond rejection with more courage. We must respond with more **belief and commitment**. Sting of a medical injection hurts bad too, but it is there to **make us better.**

Life is beautiful with all its imperfections. A poet said this very nicely

When things go wrong as they sometimes will,
　　rest if you must, but don't you quit.
When the road you are trudging seems all uphill
When the funds are low, and the debts are high

And you want to smile, but you have to sigh
When care is pressing you down a bit
Rest if you must, but don't you quit

Keep dreaming and don't let a failure fail you and use it to make yourself better. *[pause and handover control to the host]*

CHILDREN ON THE MOVE
SPEECH INTRODUCTION:
This story takes a child from Afghanistan, Pakistan, Turkey and Greece to Switzerland. This story not only shows the pain of a mother but exposes problems in our world and the challenges that our children face in our world. This story is an example of range of emotions, pauses, vocal variety and body language. This story also taught me to manage my allotted speech time. I made sure that the child reaches Turkey or Greece not too early and not too late. Too early would mean, I was speaking too fast and too late would mean that I need to pick up some pace to finish my story on time.

SPEECH BEGINS:
[Always start speech by making eye contact with one person] It was cold wintery night, in the outskirts of Kabul, Afghanistan; 12 years old Milad hugs his mom for one last time. His mother was holding him tight and would not want to let him go. *[pause and then increase pace of speech to align with action in the story]*

Milad's father grabs him by the arms, pulls him away from the clutches of his wife and starts walking outwards.

Milad departs from his home with his father holding his hands and asking his son to not look back where Milad's mother was holding on to the frame of the door, crying profusely. *(Pause to let the whole scenario play out)*

Milad's father takes him to a truck stop where he makes his final payment out of all his life savings to the "agent" *[pause],* a human smuggler. Father gives a quick kiss on his son's forehead, turns around and walks away from the truck stop, holding his head down with shame and anger, not knowing what he will tell his grieving wife, *[pause]* not knowing how what he will tell his younger children. *[pause]* Where is MILAD?

Milad is loaded into a truck, like a baggage, hiding behind bags of wheat and rice. He is scared, and he wishes if he could jump off and run back to the waiting arms of his grieving mother. *[show helplessness of the child in story through facial expressions]*

Roar of the truck's engine was the last chance he had, but he couldn't jump and then the truck departs through broken/bumpy roads in the outskirts of Kabul.

Milad crosses into Pakistan and is handed over to another agent for his future destination. While waiting for his next move, Milad goes through the struggle of learning to survive as an adult. *[pick up pace]* He starts cooking chapattis, works on gas stations, truck stops and chai shops. He gets beat up, kicked and in one case, he is offered to go to heaven for the sake of his country. *[pause]* Milad was taught by a good mother, he was determined and stays focused to his goal of reaching his own heaven called Switzerland.

After passing through Iran, Milad finds himself in Turkey and spends his nights sleeping on streets where he finds more children from his country. Calls home and tells her mother, I'm fine and everything is OK here. *[note that he is pretending as if everything is ok, it needs to show in voice]* Country is beautiful, people are rich, and no one is out to kill me. I'll soon reach Switzerland and send you some money. *[pause]*

Milad's agent takes him to Greece on a boat filled with dozens of children, the boat was overloaded, sinks very close to the shore, bodies of little children wash ashore and there are no survivors *[pause to create pain and sensation]* except one, Milad was found clinging to his life. After short medical treatment, he is sent to prison with all adults around him. Milad turns 13, an adult too soon. After few months, he is released courtesy of his agent in Greece with a promise to leave him at yet another border.

After a few months of long nights, long travel and starving days, Milad is spotted at a train station in Zurich, Switzerland wondering aimlessly. He applies for asylum and finds the heaven he waited for so long.

Calls home to mom instead talks to his dad and finds out, his mom passed away waiting to hear from his son and his younger brother and sister are now in Pakistan for their route to heaven.

[pause and make eye contact] Milad begs his father to bring back his brother and sister from Pakistan "Father, they won't make it, not many children make it, please bring them home". His father could not stop crying, it was too late. He had already sold his house and paid for their children's release to the world

with hope. *(pause to let audience absorb Milad's plea and father's helplessness)*

Milad starts his new life in Switzerland with hopes that one day he will find his siblings and father somewhere. *(pause and breathe because now you are showing Milad trying to live with hope)*

Such is the life of children on the move. *(pause and get ready for final impact and explosion of your message with power)*

My friends,

Over 50,000 children attempt to cross our southern border every year while 100s and thousands of children are taking the plunge in different parts of the world. We must support them morally, financially and politically.

[make eye contact] As adults, we may have differences, may very well have our own egos, but these children of humanity are suffering every day around the world.

Humanity's future does not have a nationality, it DOES NOT have a race, it DOES NOT have a religion and it is very colorless. *[lower your pace for the last part and pause before closing]*

A KNIGHT RIDER TRAGEDY
SPEECH INTRODUCTION:
This is one of my most favorite speeches that I did at one of my Toastmasters club. This is where I was to make a fictitious story of a company crisis where I'm expected to keep positive image of my company and answer questions from media. This is a speech where I read almost all my speech because I was to read a prepared statement.

The key to this speech was showing pain and emotion on behalf of the company. Body language and vocals were more important as opposed to eye contact because there is sense of embarrassment due to a company failure. I used following statement for introduction before my speech. Now that you have heard from Director of FBI in Orange County, CA and you have heard from Dr. King a trauma surgeon at Kaiser Permanente. I would like to invite CEO of Knight Riders Inc. to provide you his statement. He will take some of your questions after his prepared remarks. Mr. Rana.

SPEECH BEGINS:

[Make initial contact and gauge the audience] Good afternoon everyone. My name is Iqbal Rana. I'm Chairman and CEO of Knight Riders Inc. *[pause]* Yesterday was the saddest day in our company and one of very sad days for the country. As you all know yesterday at about 1:34 PDT one of the owners of our self-driving car named "KIT" went online and programmed the car to pick up her kids from school. This secure communication was intercepted by unknown hackers. After 5 minutes of the drive, hackers took control of the car and ran the car into a crowded area where unfortunately 12 people lost their lives and 8 were injured (3 of them critically and 5 had minor injuries). *[pause to show emotions]*

We are heartbroken by the loss of life and injuries to our fellow community members. I have spoken with the family members affected and I cannot begin to comprehend the pain that they are going through. I also spoke with many of programmers and architects who are smartest and brightest in what they do, but at this time they are all stunned by this development and they are all heart broken. *[pause before shifting focus and showing anger]*

This was a sabotage from a very powerful hacker that caused significant loss to human life. Currently, we do not know who is behind this attack, but our initial data logs are showing IP addresses from outside of the country. We are working closely with FBI to find out the source of attack.

Our cars are designed, manufactured and programmed within United States of America out of our facility in Aliso Viejo, CA. As a company we decided early on to ensure we do not outsource any feature or functionality to other nations. These cars are pride of USA and represent advancements of technology like none other.

These cars have been driving safely for last 5 plus years and during this time our cars were able to save 1000s of lives and millions of dollars of property damage. We were able to reduce gas consumption by 70% resulting in less dependence on foreign oil.

Having said that we knew all along about threats to our technology from hackers and we have been able to successfully foil 1000s of attempts by top hackers, in fact we have a department which is dedicated to break codes and they are incentivized to do so. This is done to make sure no one can perform criminal sabotage. Unfortunately, this specific attempt seems to be a result of activities beyond our range where we suspect espionage and significant involvement of enemies of the USA.

For this reason, FBI was engaged immediately. We are cooperating with FBI in this investigation. We have cancelled all planned vacations to ensure FBI has access to all resources any time of the day. *[pause]*

I have spoken to the President of United States and he wants to get to the bottom of this disaster as a national priority. *[pause]*

Before I close my prepared remarks, I'd like to address some speculations being made in the news media during last 24 hours about one specific incidence. The incidence, that took place two years ago where one of our self-driving cars lost control and ended up side swiping 6 cars before it hit the electric pole. Our company was cleared from this incidence after it was proven that it was an insurance fraud by a husband who was going through a bitter divorce with his wife.

[Show feistiness] I want to request all of us to show responsibility and contact with our media relations department before creating further anxiety in consumers of this technology. This is an attack by a foreign government and I will like to beg you to allow FBI to complete their investigation. We are confident about our technology and hoping that this technology will bring more safety for our next generation.

Lastly, I cannot stress enough about the pain and anguish we have as a company on the lives lost. Our thoughts and prayers are with the families of all who were affected by this sabotage. May God be with all of them during their difficult time. Now, I'll take your questions. *[pause and eye contact with each reporter asking question]*

HOLE IN YOUR POCKET

SPEECH INTRODUCTION:

This is a speech where I'm asking audience to not compete with the Joneses. Speech has humor and real-life examples to encourage audience to act and do the right thing for their well-being. This speech had more text to memorize so I highlighted key points that I talked about.

SPEECH BEGINS:

[Make an eye contact with first person of your choice and smile to start your speech] A young man came running in tears to his father. "Dad, you gave me some terrible financial advice!"

"I did? What did I tell you?" said the dad.

"You told me to put my money in that big bank, and now that big bank is in trouble."

"What are you talking about? That is one of the largest banks in the state," he said. "there must be some mistake."

"I don't think so," he sniffed. "They just returned one of my checks with a note saying, 'Insufficient Funds'."*[Allow sometime to laugh and you can smile or briefly laugh with them]*

If this happens to you, you may have a "hole in your pocket"

[Tell them what they should expect from your speech today.]

1. My objective today is to help you save money
2. My audience is anyone of you who regularly waits for pay day or has financial problems

In just five minutes, I'll show you that you have this invisible hole in your pocket. Any money that you put in, falls off and you do not even notice it.

Let me ask you,

1. Do you have home phone that never rings? *[wait for an answer from audience and asking further leading questions] -call waiting, display service, answering machine?*
2. Do you have TV channels that you never watch? *[Let someone answer this]*
3. Do you purchase pop corns and monstrous size coke at the movie theater?
4. Do you pay interest on your cards?
5. Do you have to have that latte multiple times a day?

If the answer to any of the questions above is "Yes", you have a hole in your pocket. *[pause]* If you are a middle class or below middle-class citizen, **here is a news for you,** you will never become rich. *[smile]*. This hole will keep you where you are, and it can only take you back, but never forward. This hole sometimes is quite big for upper class as well and even sinks them too. *[pause before trying to give solution]*

LEAN SIX SIGMA:

Is anyone here familiar with Lean Six Sigma philosophy at work? *[most people will not be, so it is a rhetoric question so take a short pause and move on]*

Lean Six Sigma is a philosophy that states, if you reduce defects in your process and focus on efficiency of processes, it can not only save you money, but also improve quality of your product or service, resulting in higher customer satisfaction. Lean Six Sigma talks about saving few minutes in process for one person, multiply that with number of people and number of days over a year. *[pause]*

Corporations use Lean Six Sigma to count every penny they are spending and once they realize the cost of each person and every minute of his/her work, they plug those holes by layoffs, bonus reductions, project cancellations and hiring freezes. My friends, today I'm asking if corporations can count their pennies why can we not? *[pause]*

Lean Six Sigma applies to your lives as well. If you buy a cup of latte 2 times a day 5 times a week, it adds up to 50 dollars a week, 200 dollars a month and 2400 dollars a year. You can save this money or go on a nice vacation with your loved one. <u>Remember this is not the only expense you are doing.</u>

BANK:

Are you paying mortgage interest so that you can get tax deductions? *[pause. This is a rhetoric question, so you can ask audience to raise hands if there is enough time.]*

I'm sure you know when you purchase a house, a major bulk of your interest is charged in very first few years. In many cases, you can postpone such large purchases until you have a larger down payment or if you do buy it then I suggest you pay it off as quickly as you could. If you get any extra money because of bonus or inheritance or any other way, that money if paid towards your principal during early years of your purchase can give you up to 50% return. There is no business that gives you this much return.

Don't make banks richer. Push your needs for some time and you can have an amazing life later.

TOLL ROADS:

Do you take toll roads at times when you could have easily avoided them?

I invited a friend to my house for dinner on a Saturday night, he took toll road and paid about 5 dollars to come to my house. I asked him of why he took toll road while he could have taken a freeway with not even 5 minutes of delay. His response was that he had a transponder. I had to contain my laughter. This is like someone telling you that a given restaurant is quite expensive, but I have a credit card that I can use.

Don't use the credit card or transponder if it is not your need?

LOTTERY TICKETS:

Are you a habitual lottery ticket purchaser?

If you are buying lottery tickets regularly with a hope of becoming millionaire and you have not become one yet, your probability to win will not increase in future either. If it gives you any perspective, I worked at a retail store for about 4 years where I must have sold millions of dollars' worth of tickets in my tenure, there was only winner of over 50K in 4 years.

My friends, even if you buy tickets twice a week for every lottery, do you really think that your probability increases by buying more?

Don't pay to corporations they will not be there during your rough times.

MONEY AS ART:

Making money maybe an art, but saving money is a much bigger art. It is proven from many millionaires and lottery winners that it does not take long for millions to disappear. Michael Jackson was paying 30 million dollars in interest alone. He died under debt to the tune of 400 to 500 million dollars.

CLOSING:

Remember you can never beat the Joneses, you will only be running a rat race and you can never win a rat race and as someone said, even if you do win one, you will still be a rat. *[smile]* Dave Ramsey said it best, we buy things we don't need, with money we don't have to impress people we don't like. *[smile]*

My friends, don't give it to corporations *[pause and an eye contact]*, do not follow the Joneses *[pause and an eye contact]* and keep an eye on your future. This will most definitely plug all holes in your pocket. *[pause and hand over to the host]*

MY MIDLIFE CRISES
SPEECH INTRODUCTION:
This speech is collection of publicly available jokes to make audience laugh. Key here is to use self-deprecating humor to engage audience. In this speech, true message was delivered in the middle of the speech using a sandwich approach where there are jokes before and after the message. To make audience laugh you must of course have eye contact, pauses, variety in your voice and your body should show life.

SPEECH BEGINS:
[start with statements]

* This Thursday, I'll be 45 years old. *[pause]* Or should I say, I'll be 25 with 20 years of experience? *[smile]*
* I just bought a convertible car and it sure looks nice. *[smile]*
* Other day, my wife asked me. What is wrong with you that you are doing pushups and sit ups in every corner of the house?

Every day I wake up and I'm happy to know that my wife is not pregnant and on the other hand my wife is happy to know that I might be becoming one. *[smile]*

What was going wrong with me? I was becoming a different person by the day. A childhood friend of mine suggested that I should see a doctor. Initially I thought he is advising me because he is jealous of my success, but when my son told me that I don't fit in my new convertible car. I realized that there was nothing wrong with the world and I must see a doctor. *[Pause to start the serious message]*

Upon seeing me, my doctor very quickly told me that I was going through a midlife crisis and this problem was serious.

He told me that that midlife crisis is, my current unhappiness with life and the lifestyle that may have provided me with happiness for many years.

For those who do not know, midlife age range is defined by many with different span of years; in general, midlife for both men and women starts in about 3rd quarter of average life span. This is also an age when your income peaks and you feel that you are on top of the world. You want to be noticed once again. *[Pause to complete serious message]*

In our twenties, we do not care what the world thinks of us. In our thirties we worry about what the world things of us. In our forties, we realize that nobody gives a damn about us. *[pause to let audience laugh]*. This is when we try to take control of our destiny once again

This is an age when men start worrying about how their friend have become millionaires and it's an age for women where cosmetics is not enough to make them feel younger.

The other day I was looking at LinkedIn and I saw how successful my friends are. They have become VPs, CEOs, founders and self-made millionaires. I was thinking why not me. The fact is I'm underestimating myself, if my doctor is telling me that I have midlife crisis than I must be rich because midlife crisis is a rich man's problem. *[pause]*

Midlife crises are a real thing and women are not immune to this either, they start to have body image issues more than ever before. They want to be forever 21 even if they are forty years old and have a child who is turning 18. *[smile]*

My friends, while I chose to confront my crisis for my family and friends and decided to live a simpler life. How can I tell my friend who has flat arms, but wears tight muscle shirts? *[smile]* They say the difference between a clown and a man with midlife crisis is that the clown knows he's wearing ludicrous clothes. *[smile and pause]*

How many of you know that you have a midlife crisis? *[pause, raise your hand and make eye contact with a couple of audience members]* For those of you who do not know, here are top ten signs that you may have one. *[smile and pause]*

[Show flashcards and throw them in the air one by one to create more impact. Smile after each statement]

1. You are feeling younger
2. You get a new tattoo
3. When you talk about how much a gallon of gas used to cost
4. When you must get creative about your hair
5. When cosmetic alone is not enough, and you need cosmetic surgery
6. You plan on doing a bungee jump.

7. You start doing pushups more often or Pilates if you are female
8. You buy an expensive sports car
9. Your dreams are re-runs from your past.
10. Nap time comes without warning *[may giggle]*

My friends,

The good news about midlife is that the glass is still half-full. *[pause]*, the bad news is that it won't be long before your teeth are floating in it. *[smile, pause and handover control to host]*

A MOTHER'S HUG
SPEECH INTRODUCTION:

This is an emotional speech for Mother's Day. Expectation here is to know that you will get emotional, but as a good sportsperson you should know how you will control your emotions. As a sportsperson, you will have fans at the edge of their seats and you may have played a role in invoking their emotions, but you must control your emotions to win it for them. I have seen and heard speeches where emotions whether happy or sad can sometimes take over the speech where speaker is unable to complete the speech. I never thought it would happen to me, but it did happen for an impromptu 2-minute speech where I was asked to talk about a lyric that had most impact on me. Lyrics in this case was, "We had joy, we had fun, we had seasons in the sun… Good bye Michelle my little one" I heard these lyrics after passing of my beloved young sister at the age of 18 and I used to listen to these lyrics to remember my sister. In my speech, I started the lyrics, but when I got to the word good bye, I lost it. It was my mistake, I should either not have chosen this lyric or should have stopped at the very early stages of this song. The speech remained incomplete and I had to sit for the rest of the meeting trying to control my emotions.

Following speech challenged my emotions because of how close I was to my mother, so I challenged myself to finish it gracefully. I added bullets to remember my key points and added bold fonts, uppercases and underscores to stress importance.

Lastly, while writing speech, write as such that most of your crowd can relate to the story and they can understand characters as best as possible. For example: In this story, Mary is easily understandable for some faiths, but Hajira's (mentioned as Hagar in Bible) story needs a little more elaboration. Same story may need slight alteration if faith of the audience was other way round.

SPEECH BEGINS:

[Make an eye contact with first person of your choice and start your speech]

There are two *[show two fingers]* women in the history of mankind who have shown the biggest impact on two biggest faiths in the world today. *[pause]* Both were mothers.

One was Mary, mother of Jesus, who gave birth to a child without a father. A miracle of God showing His power, followed by the pain this mother went through, in making of the Jesus. *[pause]*

Second was Hajira, wife of Abraham and mother of Ismail, who desperately ran from one hill to another in the middle of the desert in Mecca, to find food or water for a child struggling to survive. This running in desperation of a mother over 5 thousand years ago and the resulting miracle remains to be one of the biggest miracles of all times. Seeing pain of this mother, God made water appear at the heels of her son. *[pause]*

These two mothers may have been the most famous mothers of all time, but we do have our own mothers who fight for our existence from the day we are conceived. My dear mother was one of them. *[pause]* We called her *ummi*.

My mother was born in a small village in India who ultimately moved to northern province of Pakistan in very difficult circumstances possible. She married my father at a very young age where her husband was out on duties as a Pakistani soldier. When my father left army, he went to Iran and Iraq to earn living for his family. My mother remained the rock she was and helped my older brother establish a business that my father started.

1. **My mother was an illiterate person** *[pause]*, **yet she was one of the most educated persons I have known.** Her lack of education did not deter her from dreaming of her children to become doctors and engineers. She sent her two oldest daughters to complete high school where they had to commute to different town which was tremendously difficult in early seventies especially for young girls. She sent her youngest

daughter to a well-known college for her desire to do PhD where she could only stay in a boarding house. Another very extra ordinary step for a small-town mother to send her youngest daughter to a different town. My mother may have counted pennies for every little need of life, but she sent two of her sons to one of most prestigious and expensive schools in the country. She fulfilled all her dreams for her children. *[pause and move to next place and make eye contact with a different person for another point]*

2. **My mother may not have gone to school, but she was an accountant.** Every day she sat us down to count every penny in daily sale from our retail business and every penny spent by anyone in the house. This is where we not only had to justify our spends, but for her to understand business trends. *[pause and move to next place and make eye contact with a different person for another point]*

3. **My mother may not have led a corporation, but she was an executive** who strategically asked my father to buy next door house to ensure her sons have a place after they are married. She also advised on any strategic decision when it came to the business run by my father and my oldest brother. *[pause and move to next place and make eye contact with a different person for another point]*

4. **My mother may not be a saint, but she spoke with God.** She was the one who worked with my dad to save

our faith in 1974 when our family's very existence was threatened by extremist groups. *[pause]*

a. In 1986, when I was on an impossible waiting list to be readmitted to the private school and I had to temporarily go to a failing college. My mother came home one day, and she was crying. When my sister asked her of why she was crying. Her answer was that she saw someone in sherwani (my school's uniform) and she could not hold herself from asking God of why her son could not be there. I remember saying to God that if you do not listen to her then who do you listen to? I was miraculously admitted to the school after few days. *[pause]*

In her last days, there was not one single person in the house who wanted to be more than arms distance from her *[pause]* and she was terminally ill for **<u>two and a half</u>** years. *[pause]* My father wondered how he will live without her and he was trying to figure out how his life would be without her. They were an exemplary couple who could not live apart for long. My father died in a car accident 15 hours after her and was laid down next to her, so they could live happily ever after.

[It's time to close and leave a message]

My friends, *[Talk about hug by summarizing topic of my mother]*

My last long hug with my mother had to be cut short because she was too weak to continue crying. *[pause]* I still feel that hug **28** years later *[long pause]* My mother still beats in my heart. *[pause]*

Whenever I'm tested in this life, I think of my mother and how she would have spoken with God and what she would have done. *[Connect with the starting point]* My mother may not be Mary, my mother may not be Hajira, but for me she was **MY** Mary, she was **MY** Hajira. *[long pause]*

My friends

[lower voice to ask for action] If you are fortunate enough to have a mom today, she may not need your gift and she may not need flowers, but she <u>most definitely</u> needs you today.

* Your mother may not be Mary or Hajira, but she may have slept hungry while you slept with full stomach.
* You may have felt cold one day, she gave you her shawl to warm you, but she may only be getting warmth from knowing that you were warm.
* You may have slept in pain one night, but your mother may have spent all that night, <u>sleepless and in pain.</u>

Go give her a big long hug, feel the warmth of your mother, listen to her heartbeat because you never know, this hug may last a life time, like it did for me.

Happy Mother's Day everyone.

GLOSSARY

Alex Rodrigues: American professional shortstop in baseball. He played for Seattle Mariners, Texas Rangers and New York Yankees of Major League Baseball

Athlete: A person who competes in one or more sports that involve physical strength, speed or endurance

Audience: A group of listeners or spectators

Badminton: A court game played with light long handled rackets and shuttlecock volleyed over a net

Basketball: A team sport played with two teams of five players on a rectangular court with hoops at each side

Ball park: A part or stadium in which ball games (such as baseball) are played. A range (as of prices or views) within which comparison or compromise is possible

Bend it like Beckham: A 2002 British family romantic comedy sports film. The film's title refers to the football player David Beckham, and his skill at scoring from free kicks by curling the ball past a wall of defenders

Body chat: Refers to body language, nonverbal signals we use to communicate

Bullpen: A place on a baseball field where pitchers warm up before they start pitching

Clayton Kershaw: American professional pitcher in baseball. He plays for Los Angeles Dodgers of Major League Baseball

Cricket: A game played with a ball and bat by two sides of usually 11 players each on a large field centering upon two wickets each defended by a batsman

Cristiano Ronaldo: One of the top soccer (football) players of the world. He plays for country of Portugal and Real Madrid club in Union of European Football Association (UEFA)

Driving Range: An area equipped with distance markers, clubs, balls and tees for practicing golf shots

DTM: Distinguished Toastmaster – Highest public speaking and leadership title achieved at Toastmasters International

Eye on the ball: To stay focused: To continue thinking about or giving attention to something important

Fan: An enthusiastic devotee (as of sport or performing art) usually as a spectator

Football: Referred to American football played in US and Canada. This is a team sport played with two teams of eleven players on a rectangular field with goalposts at each side.

Glossophobia: Fear of public speaking or of speaking in general

Golf: A game in which a player using special clubs attempts to sink a ball with a few strokes as possible into each of the 9 or 18 successive holes on a course

Grand Slam: The winning of all four of the most significant championships in a sport in the same year – used especially in tennis and golf

Gym: Short for gymnasium: A building containing space and equipment for various indoor sports activities and usually including spectator accommodations, locker and shower rooms, offices, classrooms and a swimming pool

Home run: A hit in baseball that enables the batter to make a complete circuit of the bases and score a run

Jungle: A place of ruthless struggle for survival

Knight Rider: It was an American television series showing an artificially intelligent self-driving car which talks and helps fight crimes

Last Play: Refers to a last opportunity to ensure a win or make a big move to turn the game around

Lionel Messi: One of the top soccer (football) players of the world. He plays for country of Argentina and FC Barcelona club in Union of European Football Association (UEFA)

Max Scherzer: American professional pitcher in baseball. He plays for Washington Nationals of Major League Baseball

MLB: Major League Baseball is a professional baseball organization in North America

Midlife Crisis: A period of emotional turmoil in middle age characterized especially by a strong desire for change

Monotonous: Uttered or sounded in one unvarying tone: marked by a sameness of pitch and intensity

NBA: National Basketball Association is a professional basketball league in North America

Novak Djokovic: Professional tennis player from Serbia. He has remained number 1 player for many years and has won 14 grand slam tournaments

NSA: National Security Agency is a national intelligence agency of the United States

Pause: A temporary stop

Pitch: Degree of highness and lowness of a tone

Poker: Any of several card games in which a player bets that the value of his or her hand is greater than that of the hands held by others, in which each subsequent player must either equal or raise the bet or drop out, and in which the player holding the highest hand at the end of the betting wins the pot

Ping Pong: Another name used for sport of table tennis

Pitcher: The player who pitches (to throw to a batter) in a game of baseball

Rafael Nadal: Professional tennis player from Spain. He has remained number 1 player for many years and has won 17 grand slam tournaments

Real boss: The term is casually referred to a spouse, however more specifically for wives

Relatable: Able to be shown or established to have a causal or logical connection to something

Roger Federer: Professional tennis player from Switzerland. He has remained number 1 player for many years and has won 20 grand slam tournaments (most all times)

Ring: A square enclosure in which a fighting contest (such as a boxing or wrestling match) takes place

Serena Williams: Professional tennis player from United States of America. She has remained number 1 player for many years and has won 23 grand slam tournaments (most all times)

Sports enthusiast: Sportsperson attached to a cause or pursuit

Soccer: Also known as football outside of US and Canada. This is a team sport played with a spherical ball between two teams of eleven players with goalposts at each side

Social Animals: Animals who live in groups

Stumped: Dared or challenged

Taekwondo: A Korean art of unarmed self-defense characterized especially by the extensive use of kicks

Thanatophobia: Fear of death or dying

Tennis: A racket sport that can be played individually against a single opponent or between two teams of two players each on a rectangular court with a net in the middle

Toastmaster: A person responsible for proposing toasts, introducing speakers, and making other formal announcements at a large social event. A member of Toastmaster International club is also referred to as a toastmaster

Tone: Modulation of voice expressing a feeling or mood

Touch Down: Touching of the ground by ball behind opponent' line in sport of Rugby or American football

Tug of War: A contest in which two teams pull against each other at opposite ends of a rope with the object of pulling the middle of the rope over a mark on the ground

Usain Bolt: Sprint runner who holds the world record in 100m and 200m sprints which dubs him as fastest man on planet earth. He is from Jamaica.

Volleyball: A game played by volleying an inflated ball over a net

Wrestling: This is a combat sport involving grappling type techniques such as clinch fighting, throws and takedowns, joint locks, pins and other grappling holds

Glossary from: https://www.merriam-webster.com/

Made in the USA
Las Vegas, NV
13 June 2023